Elise Thomas Helmstetter

Self-Talk *for* Women!

Chapel
&
Croft
Publishing

Other books by Elise Thomas Helmstetter:

The Quarry—a novel

SELF-TALK FOR WOMEN

Helmstetter, Elise Thomas
    Self-Talk for Women

ISBN 1-891128-53-1

Printed in USA

10 9 8 7 6 5 4 3 2 1

Dedication

One of my earliest memories is of my mother teaching me to read. I can still see her face as we sat together, as she helped me understand the connection between the marks on the page and the meaning in my mind. Of all the many gifts she has given me, the power of words has meant the most. Without that gift, this book would not exist.

But that's only half the story. Without the work of Dr. Shad Helmstetter, there would be no story to tell. My husband Shad has given me love, support, encouragement, answers, and most of all, *understanding*—of myself and of others.

Throughout her life, my mother has been the example to me of what it means to live out the many roles we as women are called on to play: mother, daughter, sister, wife, and friend.

Shad is the one who taught me to appreciate what it takes to be all those people at once, and to do it well.

This book is dedicated with love, as it can only be, to them both.

CONTENTS

Part III

Elise Thomas Helmstetter

Self-Talk
for
Women!

Chapel
&
Croft
Publishing

Introduction
by Shad Helmstetter, Ph.D.

T he book you hold is a remarkable work, written by a remarkable woman. This woman is Elise Thomas Helmstetter, and she has "been there and done that." The first time I saw Elise, she was wearing full head-to-toe "night-fighter" military camouflage. Her short, dark hair was tucked under a beret, and because her face was blackened with black and green face paint, all I could really see were the whites of her eyes. The rest of her outfit, complete with all-black clothing, boots, and a 9MM pistol tucked into her belt, suggested that here was a woman one should take seriously.

Although Elise was wearing the military outfit as a costume for a Toys-for-Tots Halloween charity event, it turned out that both she and the outfit she wore were the real thing. Just a short time before we met, Elise had been named "Soldier of the Year" out of more than 145,000 US military troops—men and women—in Europe. She was a dedicated and decorated soldier who rose to the top through determination and fortitude.

People who meet her at a seminar or see her on television might have a hard time imagining that Elise was once a soldier; she is the essence of womanhood. She is also a brilliant student of the classics, an exceptional novelist, a truly inspiring and motivating speaker, and with this book, a new-found friend to everyone who reads the pages that follow. And I should add that this unstoppable woman is also my wife.

For you, the reader, let me share with you one small, but typical, snapshot of Elise, and in so doing show you the kind of "attitude" this book has in store for you.

During the time Elise was soldiering, her military company often had to go through a difficult series of physical endurance tests. Some, like Elise, made it through the forced runs, rope climbing, obstacle courses, and grueling physical exercises. But others lacked the strength, or the determination to succeed.

When that happened, Elise would circle back, run in step with the ones who had fallen behind, and talk and shout them through to the finish. When a struggling comrade was unable to do one more push-up, Elise was there, on the ground beside her, whispering, encouraging, refusing to let her give up, helping her teammate find the strength to make it through.

In the years since, whether she is teaching and motivating an audience of thousands, writing a book, or encouraging a friend, that same enthusiasm and spirit shines through. She successfully manages a busy life of traveling throughout the world, being a businesswoman, somehow always finding time for her family, and never failing to care about *you*.

When it comes to living out the kind of life and reaching the kind of goals that elude so many, Elise has been there, she has done that—and she has won. In your own life, with your own goals, she will help you do the same.

Throughout the time that I wrote a number of books on the subject of Self-Talk, I knew that *no one* but a woman, and a very qualified woman at that, could write a book about Self-Talk *for women*. Elise is that woman. After studying and teaching the subject of Self-Talk for nearly ten years, and living it for herself, Elise has written the finest—and best—book on Self-Talk thus far. This one is written *by* a woman, *for all* women. This one is for you.

Shad Helmstetter, Ph.D.

Part I
SELF-TALK FOR WOMEN

*Imagine yourself
the way you are
when you're having
a great day.*

*Now imagine yourself
having days like that
a lot more often.*

That's what Self-Talk does.

Chapter 1

WHAT THIS BOOK IS ABOUT, AND WHAT IT CAN DO FOR YOU

*Y*ou never know when something you say or do can make a critical difference in the life of another person. For me, that happened in the form of an encouraging message from a friend, telling me what I needed to hear about myself at a time in my life when I most needed to hear it. My friend may never quite know the impact those words had on me, but I keep them close at hand, engraved on my memory, to replay to myself in times of need.

Among other things, my friend told me I was very special, that time spent with me was always time well spent, and that I had the ability to reach my dreams. Because of a few simple but important words at exactly the right time, I felt loved, validated, and *appreciated* for who I am. What a gift for one friend to give another!

That incident was only one example of the thousands of

little things that happen to all of us, one of the countless moments that make up the course of a life. I could have gone right past the moment, and not thought another thing about it, as we often do—but instead, I stopped and thought about it. To me, it was much more than an insignificant bit of time that would be almost immediately forgotten, because in that moment, my friend's words made a real difference.

What mattered most is the fact that I listened, paid attention to the meaning behind the words, and *held onto* that special message. I took strength from it, gratefully accepted the mental lift, and was able to get on with my life in a happier and more confident frame of mind.

That simple circumstance brought home to me, in a way nothing else quite could, the impact of what happens to each of us in the course of our everyday lives.

We *all* need to hear that we are special, and important, and loved, and appreciated for who we are. But all too often, we don't get to hear those crucial words—and sometimes, we even have trouble *believing* the good things people say to us, about us, when we *do* hear them.

WHY DOES IT HAVE TO BE
SO DIFFICULT?

We all face challenges, and the challenges we face as women today are especially difficult for many of us. We live in a world that seems designed to destroy our dreams, sap our self-confidence, and diminish our self-belief. And many of us feel there's very little we can do about it.

But *why* do we hurt? Why do we struggle, and why do we give in to the doubts and the fears and the feelings that no matter how hard we try, we can never quite measure up? Why does it have to be so difficult to love ourselves and appreciate our own good points, when others can clearly see our value and worth? And what, if anything, can we do about it?

That's what this book is for.

THERE *IS* SOMETHING YOU CAN DO

I've learned something about why life can be so difficult. I've discovered something that can help you get *past* those stumbling blocks between you and the person you were meant to be.

I have found that there *is* a method that can help you become that confident, contented woman living the kind of life you may have imagined belongs only to a lucky few, but never to you.

The solution I'm talking about, when properly applied to your life, will make a dramatic difference in every moment of every day you live. It is an answer that is particularly effective for women, because it deals with *how* and *why* you have become the way you are, why you sometimes feel life is a struggle, and what you can do about it.

It's a method that not only can *change* your life in very positive ways, but can also help you to better understand and appreciate the life you *already* have.

This book is about a major breakthrough in personal growth and human awareness. The breakthrough is called Self-Talk, and it has to do with the way your computer-like brain turns everyday "messages" into strong mental *"programs"* that affect literally every area of your life. But don't worry—I promise not to make it difficult to understand. I even hope to convince you of the opposite: that learning about Self-Talk can be effective, easy to do, interesting, and *exciting*.

My purpose in writing this book is to share with you what I have learned about Self-Talk and how to use it, because I am convinced that it will help you live a happier and more fulfilling life.

YOU'RE NOT IN IT ALONE

With any good book, there is a kind of trust established between the writer and the reader, and this book is no exception. Throughout the book, my goal is to let you know in every way I can that I genuinely *care* about helping you understand and apply what you learn. You're investing your valuable time to read this book, and you deserve to know that you can trust the integrity and quality of what you are about to read.

We may not have met in person, at least not yet, but if we could meet face to face, I hope and believe you would see the right look in my eyes—the look that says, "I'm here to help you, because it *matters* to me what you think and how you feel. I know what it feels like to hurt, to worry, to struggle and fail *and not know why*—and I'd like to share with you a way to make it better."

I assure you I've done everything in my power to tell you what I know to be true, in a way you can understand and believe in and trust. Your life is important to you, and helping you make it better is important to me. That's what I do; that's the kind of woman *I* am.

WHO I AM, AND WHY I'M HERE

Ever since I was a little girl, I have wanted to help other people, to cheer them up or at least make them smile.

My mother likes to tell the story of how her four-year-old daughter made her laugh at a difficult moment during a cross-country bus trip. We were stuck at a Greyhound station in the middle of nowhere in the middle of the night, and Mom was exhausted from trying to corral me and my three older sisters all by herself. She was ready to quit or cry (she says she's not sure which) when someone put a quarter in the juke box.

As the music filled that run-down, dirty bus station, her skinny brown-haired baby girl with the crooked bangs (me) went bouncing up to her and said loudly, *"It's time to dance!"*

I can't claim that at four years of age I knew what I was doing well enough to have done it on purpose, but I *did* cheer her up. And as I grew, I didn't change all that much.

I'm the one who adopts stray pets and people, the one

who will talk to a total stranger in an airport because she's crying and I can't stand to walk away and leave her hurting if there's anything I can do about it. I will usually wind up with her life story, her address, and a promise to write, before we hug each other goodbye. I'm still the one who wants to make people feel good, about themselves and about life.

TURNING YOUR DREAMS INTO REALITY

As you may have figured out by now, I'm not shy. I like people, and I could no more stop caring about others than I could go through life without hot fudge. (In fact, just to set the record straight, I won the county spelling bee when I was twelve because my sixth-grade teacher had promised me "the biggest hot fudge sundae I had ever seen" if I won, *not* because of any natural talent on my part. Besides, she was counting on me. I practiced for *days*. It was worth it. The picture in the local paper showed me, still skinny, still with bad bangs *and* dumb eyeglasses, *the winner*—with my ice cream. And Miss Sutton, wherever you are, it's *still* the biggest hot fudge sundae I've ever had.)

At twelve, I had no idea that what I had done to win that spelling bee was to set a goal with a worthwhile reward, make a plan, and follow the action steps necessary to reach the goal. I didn't even know what a goal *was*, much less how to reach one. I was just dreaming of ice cream.

My haircut looks better now (except when I first wake

up), and thanks to laser surgery I no longer have to wear bad glasses. And after a long time and a lot of hard work, I eventually learned how to turn a *dream* into an achievable *goal*.

Whether reaching my goal to help people involves flying for 18 hours straight to speak to an audience in Australia, traveling by train to a city in Poland to spread the word of self-worth and personal growth, or holding public seminar programs to tell women what they can achieve and what they can become, the effort it takes is more than worthwhile.

The same holds true for this book. If I had known the incredibly demanding amount of hard work, prayer, energy, discussion, editing, and rewriting it would take to make the book a reality, I'm still convinced I would have done it anyway. Whatever it took, *it was worth it*—because I know from years of experience the kind of positive changes that await you in your life if you understand and apply the message of how Self-Talk works.

You are not
forever tied
to the way it <u>is</u>,
just because
that's the way
it has always <u>been</u>.

Chapter 2

Is There Anything in Your Life You Would Like to Change?

*W*herever you are right now, whatever you're doing while you read this book, take a moment and raise your hand if there's anything about you or your life you'd like to change.

Really? I had a feeling that might be the case. And by the way, if you actually raised your hand, whether or not anyone gave you a funny look when you did it, I promise that's as embarrassing as this process will get. What you choose to change is nobody's business but yours; if there's one thing we women today are short of, it's *privacy*. Feel free to keep your ideas to yourself on this, unless and until you choose to share them with anyone.

That includes your husband, your parents, your minister or rabbi or priest, your kids, and your pet. If you have a dog, he already loves you anyway—and I know from personal experience that if you have a cat, she couldn't

14

care less.

Oh, and one other thing: just in case your husband or your father or your son or your special "someone" is looking over your shoulder as you read this—or has borrowed this book from you to find out what's going on inside that female mind of yours—there's something you should know. The fact that you might want to make some changes, even positive ones, could make them a little bit nervous or uncomfortable.

Go ahead and let them off the hook. Let them know the truth up front: learning about Self-Talk and how to use it is a *good* thing.

SELF-TALK IS DESIGNED
TO IMPROVE THEIR LIVES, TOO

Self-Talk is designed to help you create and maintain *better* relationships, *not* to jeopardize the relationships you already have. Your friends and loved ones need not worry that you will suddenly change beyond recognition, just because you've made the choice to learn something new that will help you feel better about yourself and help you be more effective in the life you are living.

It's important that you take the time and effort to reassure the people who are closest to you that you'll still be the woman they know and love when you finish the book—only better! Just tell them to imagine you the way you are when you're having a totally great day. Then tell them to imagine you having a lot more days like that, a lot more often. That's what Self-Talk does.

If the men in your life are anything at all like most men, they'll pray you keep reading!

(If all else fails—if they still don't understand, or they keep asking you about the book, and you can't think of anything else to say—tell them it's a sure-fire method for curing PMS. It works every time; men are *guaranteed* to change the subject.)

SELF-TALK WORKS FOR EVERYONE
AND WORKS *ESPECIALLY* WELL FOR WOMEN

Self-Talk techniques have been proven effective for all kinds of people, from preschool children to members of the clergy, from wives and mothers to people in the professions of law, science, and medicine. Self-Talk works for everyone, and it can work for you, no matter what kind of woman you are.

Are you the kind of woman that tends to take charge of managing every detail of your life? Self-Talk can help you do that. And if you're the one who somehow winds up keeping everyone *else* around you on track, almost in spite of them, you might learn some new ways to stay in control without losing your sanity!

If, on the other hand, you're a quiet person who is inclined to nurture others before taking time for yourself, you'll find that the right new Self-Talk techniques can bring you added strength and peace of mind. Sharing what you learn with others may even help them figure out how you remain calm when everyone around you is upset.

16

Does clear, factual information make a difference to you? If you're a thoughtful woman, who prefers to analyze every detail of any new information that comes your way, the structure and medical credibility of Self-Talk will appeal to you. The methods presented to you in this book have stood up to more than fifteen years of intense scrutiny from medical doctors, therapists, educators, neuroscientists, and other professionals around the globe. Self-Talk works, and the results prove that it does.

If you're a bright, bubbly, life-of-the-party person, and talk about science and proof leaves you cold, remember this: discovering Self-Talk can be fascinating! It's great fun to see yourself making changes in your life when you figure out you don't have to be stuck in the same old rut. If you're a cheerful person with plenty of energy, you'll really enjoy yourself with this.

A SIMPLE METHOD THAT *WORKS*

No matter who you are, or *how* you are, Self-Talk gives you the method and the tools you need to take on the challenges in your life, and win—and feel better about yourself in the process. There are as many unique ways to put Self-Talk to work in your life as there are women who want to improve. How you choose to apply the techniques you're about to learn will be up to you.

Nothing you read here will be difficult to understand or follow. The most important aspect of any good self-improvement method is *simplicity*. If it takes too much time, asks you to make changes that are too drastic, or otherwise adds a burden to your life, *it won't work.*

You won't find anything like that here. Everything you're about to learn, every small but important new step you're about to take, has been done before by countless individuals just like you.

Just because learning how to use new Self-Talk is fun and easy, however, doesn't mean it won't work. If what I have to tell you ever sounds too simple, remember: the process *is* very simple—but the results are not.

Wave your wand.

Make your list.

*No matter what
your goals are,
Self-Talk can help you
achieve them.*

Chapter 3

SELF-TALK GETS RESULTS

 *W*e are fortunate that we live in a time when technology is making incredible advances on an almost daily basis. And it is true that the current *proof* of Self-Talk comes from recent advances in the field of medical computer technology.

But the *idea* behind the techniques I'm going to teach you in this book is older than computers, and almost as old as mankind itself. This idea is so old and time-honored, in fact, that it is talked about in the Bible.

You may be familiar with the Biblical quote that reads, "As a man thinketh in his heart, so is he." And it makes sense to believe that we are a product of our thoughts; we've known that for a long time.

By now, most people know that "positive thinking" is important to anyone who wants to live a successful life. What many people don't realize, however, is that the truth about the way our minds work goes much deeper than just "thinking positive."

It's easy to *tell* someone to be more optimistic or less negative—but that doesn't help. In fact, it often just makes things worse. It's frustrating.

Most people *would* like to be more positive, and do better in their lives, if they could figure out how. But life somehow keeps getting in the way of those good intentions, sabotaging great ideas and sincere efforts, putting people right back into the same old thoughts and habits that held them back in the first place.

For a long time, it seemed like nothing helped. Nobody could figure out a way to make positive, lasting changes in people's lives. There were many good ideas, and some of them worked for a while, but eventually, the old negative patterns would come back. No one could find a simple method that actually *worked*, and *kept* working—until now.

THE ONE WHO GAVE US
A SIMPLE ANSWER

Why *do* some people succeed and others fail, even when they are faced with very similar situations? Why *can* someone set a goal and be absolutely determined to make a positive change this time, only to slip back into the old habits after a few days?

The reason the best-intentioned motivators in the world could help people, but only *for a short time*, is that they only had half the answer. They had the right idea when they told people to be more positive, and they could even get people excited and motivated for a time. But the other half, the key to making the changes *last*, eluded them—because the motivators were looking for the answer *in the wrong place*.

As it turns out, the missing element of the solution came from science. The key was found in the laboratories where neuroscientists were studying the way the human brain works, in an effort to cure Alzheimer's disease and other brain disorders.

In his book, *What To Say When You Talk To Your Self*, Dr. Shad Helmstetter explains how he put the field of motivational psychology *together* with the research on the study of the brain, in order to come up with a *lasting* solution to behavioral change. He took a great deal of research on two vastly complicated and different subjects, and came up with a simple process for changing lives—*permanently*.

The answer he discovered is what we now call Self-Talk, and the popular application of Self-Talk has changed thousands of lives for the better.

I know I'm *supposed* to say good things like that, since Dr. Helmstetter is also my husband—but it's more than personal bias that has made me such a strong believer in his work. It's the *results* that convinced me.

WHAT SELF-TALK HAS DONE
FOR PEOPLE I KNOW

For nearly a decade, I've had the privilege to witness firsthand the results of Self-Talk in this country and around the world. I've seen the changes people have made in their lives, changes that range from the dramatic to the simple, from losing weight to creating a whole new career and becoming financially free.

Because of Self-Talk, Marilyn gained back a daughter she thought was lost to drugs and alcohol.

Because of Self-Talk, my friend Tracy is able to keep her sanity while living in a household with her husband and a teenage son who both suffer from attention deficit disorder.

Because of Self-Talk, Debie is able to share a message of hope in prisons across her state as she teaches inmates how to rebuild their self-belief and their lives.

Because of Self-Talk, Marie has found a way to teach self-esteem to her class of third-grade students in spite of lack of funding and an overcrowded classroom.

Because of Self-Talk, a nine-year-old boy named Billy was able to write a letter of thanks because he is no longer afraid of the dark.

Because of Self-Talk, Karen has gained the confidence to move to a different city, change her job, and enjoy a lifestyle rich in the things she values most: her family, her cat, her garden, and her church.

. . . and the list goes on.

WHAT SELF-TALK HAS DONE
FOR ME

I've seen Self-Talk change countless lives—and I've seen it change mine. I've always been a person who *wanted* to do my best, who *wanted* to achieve. But until I learned to apply the techniques of positive Self-Talk you'll learn in this book, my life was far more difficult than it needed to be.

I argue less now than I used to. I am a calmer person, because I have learned Self-Talk methods for reducing stress that really work.

I fought a battle with my weight for most of my life (the hot fudge again!). Thanks to Self-Talk, I am finally able to follow the rules of a healthy diet and plenty of exercise, so my body stays in much better shape.

As a young person, I never had much faith in relationships, since it seemed to me at times that my own parents were almost the only ones I knew who got married and stayed that way. Most of my friends had half- or step-brothers and sisters, along with multiple sets of "parents." By applying Self-Talk to the area of my personal relationships, I have built confidence that I *can* have a solid relationship that will last.

It would take too long to list for you all the specific ways in which Self-Talk has impacted my life. I'll be sharing more instances of that throughout the book—but as you can see from even these few examples, I'm speaking from personal experience when I tell you that Self-Talk works.

WHAT SELF-TALK CAN DO FOR *YOU*

Whatever your situation is, Self-Talk can help you

improve it. Whatever changes you would like to make in your life, Self-Talk can help you make them. Whatever failures or disappointments you have faced in the past or are still trying to deal with, Self-Talk can help you turn them into success.

Wave your wand. Make your list. Big or small, short-term or lifelong, no matter what the goal is, Self-Talk can help you achieve it.

If it sounds like Self-Talk is powerful, that's because it is. If I sound confident about what Self-Talk can do, that's because I get the letters. I hear the personal stories. I see the pictures of lives that are *different*—and *better*—because someone took the time to learn how to apply Self-Talk in a practical, solid, day-to-day manner.

SELF-TALK FOR WOMEN
IN TEN EASY LESSONS

In the pages that follow, I've distilled fifteen years of research into a few short chapters. If you read carefully and pay close attention for the next short while, you will gain access to a powerful technique that can help you make literally any change you choose to make.

In this book, I have explained in clear simple terms how to apply the discovery of Self-Talk to your own life. You'll learn what Self-Talk is, how it works, why it matters, and how to apply it.

I recommend that you take your time on this part, and make sure you understand each point clearly before you move on to the next. It's worth it.

You'll know when you see a key point, because they're numbered and highlighted and it will say **"Key Point"** in large bold print right next to the part it's important for you to know.

After you go through the process of understanding all about Self-Talk, you'll get to the sections where you'll learn specific Self-Talk to use in each of the main areas of your life.

You'll also have the opportunity to take a look at where you are now, and where you would like to go next with your life. In order to do that, let's first take a look at where you've been—from the beginning.

Let's see what happened the day you were born.

Anytime you tell another person
anything,
remember this:

You're typing programs
into that person's keyboard.

What you say,
if repeated often enough,
will be acted on
as if it's *true.*

What kind of programs
are you typing in?

Chapter 4

The Basics of Programming

*W*hen you arrived on the planet Earth, as a newborn infant, you were helpless. You were completely dependent on your parents, especially your mother, for everything from food and water to warmth, comfort and love.

That was true of each of us. We've known for a long time that as children, we were dependent on our parents for our physical needs. What we *didn't* know until recently is that each of us was also depending on our parents for something as important in the long term as the food and water we would have died without. We were depending on our parents to give us our *programs*.

Key Point #1:
From the moment you were born, your computer-like brain got programmed by hearing messages about you.

We've learned that the human brain works much like a powerful personal computer. Your brain has stored all your programs by recording them in your mind, regardless of who they came from. And the programs were stored in your subconscious mind, *whether the words about you were true at the time, or not.*

"TELL ME WHO I AM . . ."

It is as if, when you arrived into this world, you had a tiny computer keyboard strapped to your little chest, facing outward. You couldn't speak yet, but if you could have, you would have held your keyboard out to the world around you and said:

"Here, Mom; here, Dad; here, world—would you please tell me about myself? Would you give me strength and courage, and teach me kindness and how to have a positive attitude? And would you mind typing in some self-belief, so I won't have to struggle with that later on?

"While you're at it, would you let me know how smart I am and how capable I can be? Oh, and by the way—*whatever you type into my little keyboard will be stored for the rest of my life, and will determine exactly what I'll become* . . . so I hope you're really good at this, because I have no choice but to take what you give me. The programs you give me, about *me*, will set the course for who I become and what I can do with my life.

"We have a few years together to work on this programming thing, Mom and Dad, so let's get started right away, okay? Go ahead: *tell me who I am!*"

I'm not saying we were, or are, anything like computers or robots; nothing I say here is meant to imply anything

29

of the kind. But we have discovered beyond a doubt that it is true: we, as humans, get *programmed* from birth—perhaps even from before birth—with a nonstop series of messages that eventually determine how well we do at anything we try.

The important point here is that *everything* that has ever been said to us, about us, has been stored for *life, permanently,* in our subconscious minds, like a computer stores its programs on a hard drive or a floppy disk. This is true regardless of what the message was, who it came from (ourselves, or others), what it was about, and *whether it was true about us at the time or not.*

All of the programs just got stored!

AS A FEMALE, WHAT KIND OF PROGRAMS DID YOU GET?

What kinds of things were said to you as you grew up? What kind of programs did you get? What do you remember being told about yourself by your parents, your brothers and sisters, then by the kids at school, and by your teachers and boyfriends and friends?

The people around you meant well. They just didn't know what they were doing when they said things like, *"You don't have a brain in your head,"* or *"You'll never get a date because you've always got your nose buried in a book,"* or *"You're just a little chatterbox, aren't you—all mouth and no ears!"*

Some of the most devastating programs of all are the ones that included your own name as part of the equation. Kids in particular seem to be much too good at finding the sore spots.

For example, one of my best friends, Patricia, refuses to be called by the nickname of Pat or Patty, because as a child, she was taunted with calls of "fatty Patty." The other kids liked the way it rhymed, I suppose, and they could see it bothered her.

She was a self-described "pudgy kid" whose mom shopped in the "chubby" section for all her clothes. Just think of the kind of programs *that* gave her!

Years later, my friend's old programs of insecurity and self-doubt gave rise to a life-threatening struggle with bulimia.

She eventually managed to get through it by changing her old programs with Self-Talk, as well as finding a new set of adult friends who believed in her and repeatedly told her so. Today, my friend is one of the most personally effective professional women I've ever met. She now spends her time teaching Self-Talk concepts to others, helping them get past their old programs and get on with their lives.

The reason it is difficult, the reason we struggle with the effects of what we've believed about ourselves all these years, is that unless we do what it takes to change them, those seemingly innocent messages about us *never go away.*

IT'S ALL STILL THERE

Every program you've ever received is still there.

It is easy to show how true this is; just take a moment and think back to a time in your early life when someone said something important to you, about you. It could be something good, or something you'd just as soon erase from your memory.

No matter what it was—and most of us can think of all too many things we were told—chances are that the entire memory is still there. And there's only one way that could be true: if it were *recorded* in your mind.

Key Point #2:
Each message you've ever gotten about you as a woman has been *physically* recorded in chemical pathways in your brain.

The patterns are physical, and they are really there. Through the use of medical computer imaging technology, neuroscientists can actually watch the brain work *while it is working*—and by now, they can even see pictures of your programs in action.

That's the most complicated part of the Self-Talk picture, but it is also the most exciting. With the answers they've found through their research, the neuroscientists proved beyond a doubt that Dr. Helmstetter's theory about programming was accurate.

Dr. Helmstetter knew from his research of studying people and their actions that programming existed, and he had found through observation that people got programmed through repeatedly hearing the same messages over and over, or repeating similar experiences again and again. But it took the medical community several more years to prove what he knew to be true.

It's not necessary that you understand the process by

which the brain physically records every input you get. What matters is that you get the picture that programs are very real, that they are a physical and chemical part of you, and that they are created by what you hear, think, say, see, imagine, or experience in any way.

TAKE A WALK IN "SELF-TALK PARK"

The first time you received a message that told you something about yourself, it probably didn't make much of an impression. But if that same program was repeated again, by that same person or by your own mind repeating the words back to yourself, the program got stronger. And that simple repeating and recording process is the basis of many of our troubles. The good news is, the same process also holds the key to our success. It works like this.

Picture a field of grass, a smooth field with no paths across it. The first time you receive a program message about you is like the first time you walk across the grass—it doesn't leave much of an imprint. You can hardly see the impression.

Then imagine you go that same way again. The message gets repeated, and when it does, it follows *the same chemical pathway* in your brain. The path in the grass gets more noticeable.

Every time you walk over the path—every time you hear the same thing, or think the same thing, or say the same thing, or *do* the same thing, again—the pathway gets deeper, and wider.

IF YOU GET THE SAME PROGRAM OFTEN ENOUGH, IT BECOMES TRUE ABOUT YOU

The first time you were told something about you, it didn't make much of a mark. But if you heard that same remark or something similar again, it made more of an impression. Each time it was repeated, you got a stronger program.

A good example of this is the way many of us put on extra pounds as we were growing up. For instance, the first time you were told something like, "Cheryl, you're going to be big, like your dad's side of the family," you might not even have been old enough to know what you were hearing. There wasn't much of a program yet.

But as you grew, if you heard it again, and again, that same message got bigger and bigger in your mind—and as it did, you probably got bigger and bigger in your body at the same time. Even if it wasn't *genetically* true at all, even if you were born to be naturally thin, your eating habits followed the path laid out for you by your programs about how you were "supposed" to look.

The strength of that repeated program, and others like it, built a highway in your mind that took your life and your body in the wrong direction.

Eventually, what you heard about you most is what you began to become.

Key Point #3:
Through repetition of the same message over and over, some program paths get stronger than others.

The repeated paths use more cells, they are physically fed more nutrition, and they continue to grow every time the same message is repeated.

With repeated use, what was once a simple path becomes a country lane, then a road, then a highway, and then a *super*highway in your brain. And each program has its own highways to follow. By whatever age you are now, your brain is like a road map filled with small roads and highways and huge interstate expressways of programs you've gotten throughout your life.

The process never stops, because every time you travel one of those program highways by repeating the same thought or saying the same words or repeating the same experience, you literally *feed* that program path by sending nutrition to those particular brain cells.

Sometimes, it only takes a single strong program message from an authority like a parent or a teacher to create a superhighway.

Anytime a strong emotion is present, like when a parent yells at a child, or when you're really hoping to hear something good about yourself and you hear the opposite instead, the recording process goes into overdrive. Whatever is said next will set a clear, strong pattern. The trouble is, the superhighways all too often lead in the exact wrong direction of the destination you would choose for yourself.

IT STARTS WHEN YOU'RE A LITTLE GIRL,
AND IT NEVER STOPS

Not long ago, my husband and I were giving a Self-Talk presentation to an audience of several thousand people in California. A woman, who I will call Amy, told us the story of how her entire life had been affected by a program she received when she was a little girl.

When Amy was seven or eight years old, she was watching the Little Miss America pageant on television one day.

"All the little girls were up there on that stage in their beautiful dresses—they looked like princesses to me," she said. "I wanted more than anything in the world to be like them, to be pretty and graceful, like a ballerina. Just then my father came into the room and saw what I was watching. He looked at the contestants, then at me, and said, 'If that was you, Amy, you'd probably trip!'"

HER FATHER DIDN'T KNOW
HIS WORDS MADE A DIFFERENCE

Nearly thirty years later, Amy was still trying to live a life that would repair the damage from that remark, and countless others like it, that had painted a clear and believable, but entirely *untrue*, picture of herself in her mind as a clumsy, unbeautiful, unlovable person who couldn't do anything without messing it up.

Amy's father, of course, had no idea of the impact of his words. If asked, he probably would have said that everything he said to his daughter just "went in one ear and out the other."

But we know now that it isn't true, and it never was

true to begin with. The words came in—but they didn't just go out the other side. They stopped in the middle, and were *programmed permanently* into her subconscious mind.

One of the most interesting things about Amy's story to me was that to look at her, you would instantly get the impression of a lovely, slender, graceful woman who would probably do well at anything she tried. She was financially and professionally successful, and had eventually developed a strong and happy marriage—but none of it had come easily to her.

Throughout her life, Amy had struggled with the legacy of a "gift" she was given as a young girl, from a man who had no idea what he was taking away from his daughter in that moment. And like Amy, each of us is the recipient of program after program like that one.

IT'S NOT JUST WHAT YOU *HEAR;* IT'S *EVERY* PROGRAM YOU GET

It might not be as important if the programs we got were limited to what others *said* to us, but it's more complex than that. The programming process was built into all humans to protect us from danger and to help us learn, so we're designed to get programs from *all* of our senses, not just from what we hear.

A single look from someone can communicate volumes to you about you. Whether the person giving the look is a parent, a brother or sister, a boyfriend or husband or one of your children, the message is communicated without words—but *it still gets programmed in.*

Even your senses of smell and taste are used to create programs, and in fact, they are associated with some of your *strongest* programs. It's easy to see how true that is; just think back to the most recent time a familiar taste or smell called up an entire memory from your past.

You get programmed by what people say to you and what they *don't* say, by the way you are touched—or *not* touched, by the way people look at you, by the smiles or frowns you get—even when that other person is thinking about something that has nothing to do with you whatsoever!

The important point here is that *every* input you get, from *any* source, becomes a *program*—and those programs stay with you.

IT STARTS WITH OUR PARENTS, BUT IT ENDS WITH US

We've learned what happens when *other* people give us a program about ourselves. It starts with our parents and our teachers and our so-called friends. And if that's as far as it went, it probably wouldn't have the impact on us that it does.

If that's all there were to it, most of us would have the ability to get past the outside input we get. We would more than likely be able to get on with our lives without consciously dwelling on the negative or unpleasant things that were said to us, about us, while we were growing up.

The reason we fail, the reason we are held back and

have to try so hard, is that our negative programs *begin* with what other people tell us and with the way other people treat us, but the programs don't *stop* there.

WHEN "YOU" BECOMES "I"

The *real* power of programming is what happens when *we* take over. What makes the strongest programs are the messages we give ourselves. And unless we know how the programming process works, and how to take control of it, *our own* programs do the greatest damage of all.

Do you think Amy's father ever had to repeat his hurtful words to her again for her to replay that scene over and over in her mind?

No. And each time she repeated his words to herself, she made that program pathway stronger than ever.

Every time Amy made a normal, natural mistake, or showed the slightest sign of clumsiness, she saw that as proof that her father had been right about her.

His words rang out again and again in her mind, telling her she was no good, she wasn't capable, she shouldn't try or she might stumble or fall. She would *fail* . . . and somewhere along the line, for Amy and for each of us, the word "*you*" started to get replaced with the word "*I*."

When that change happened, when you first began to say things to yourself and to other people like "*I* can't do it," or "*I* don't think I'm good enough," you became the one most in charge of what happened to you next. Whether you realized it or not, you became the strongest source of your own programs.

TAKING CONTROL OF YOUR KEYBOARD

Until now, you might not have known about your mental programs and how they work. But when you know how the programming process works, you can make it work in your favor.

Self-Talk is designed to help you do that. Self-Talk is a potentially life-changing process of taking your computer keyboard *back* from the world around you, so that never again will you passively accept the wrong program information about yourself.

From now on, *you* get to determine what kind of messages are typed in. It's time to type in some newer, better programs of your own—and by the time you finish this book, you'll know exactly how to do that. I will show you how to put Self-Talk into practice by making a few simple changes in what you do each day, to create the long-term results you want.

In any situation,
you either have more programs
that vote _for_ you,
or more programs
that vote _against_ you.

The key to making your life
work better
is to change that balance
so the strongest programs
you get
will always vote
in your favor.

Chapter 5

WHY YOU DO WHAT YOU DO

I f you could hook up a computer printer to your subconscious mind and push a button to print out a list of all your programs, what would you find out about yourself? What would a printout of your programs look like, if you could read it? Would you even *want* to read it, by now? Most of us probably wouldn't.

We can't hook up that printer, but you *can* get a fairly accurate idea of what your programs are right now.

WHAT DO *YOUR* OLD PROGRAMS SOUND LIKE?

When you speak, you reveal your programs. If you want to know what your programs are, *listen to what you say*—and especially what you are saying about yourself.

Some time ago, Dr. Helmstetter wrote and published a

list he called the "Hot 100." It was a kind of program printout of the things people say out loud about themselves, and it was almost startling to read. Most people were surprised to recognize how counter-productive many of their own words were.

But how did it happen? You weren't born saying "*I can never win.*" So how did you get from that innocent, newborn baby girl with a world of potential in front of you to who and where you are now?

Someone *else* gave the wrong programs to you first, and your brain believed them, because the part of your brain that stores your programs does only that. It stores them. The subconscious mind, your personal floppy disk, doesn't know what is true and what is false about you. It's just a recording device.

If you were told something often enough, or if you experienced something often enough, you began to believe it—and more important, to *repeat* it on your *own*.

What do *your* programs sound like? What are you saying about yourself without even knowing you're doing it? Do most of your programs currently work *for* you, or against you?

THE "HOT 100" FOR WOMEN

I've tailored the following list of program statements to reflect what I hear women say most often about themselves. Take a moment and see if you might say any of the same kinds of things. If you do, make a check mark next to the ones that hit home, or keep a separate list of the pertinent statements that sound like you—because what you're seeing and hearing is your own personal programs in action.

Here's the list:

The "Hot 100" for Women

I'm having a bad hair day.
I'm no good at math.
I'm not smart enough for college.
I'm so tired.
My memory isn't what it used to be.
My sister got all the looks in the family.
I'm a chocoholic.
I used to look good—but then I had kids.
I'm at my wits' end.
I'm too short.
I have thunder thighs.
I can never keep a secret.
Nobody listens to me.
My kids control my life.
I'm out of control!
I just can't help myself.
I'm fat.
I'm not pretty.
I'm so disorganized.
I never seem to get around to it.
I'm no good at talking in front of a group.
I can't do anything right.
I'll never make it.
I can't get a date.
I'm a bad mother.

What difference does it make?
My opinions don't really matter.
I'm so far behind I'll never catch up!
If I want something done right, I have to do it myself.
It's making me crazy.
My life is going nowhere.
I hate my job.
I have too much to do.
I have no time for myself.
The kids come first.
My husband would never let me do that.
I can never keep my house clean.
I'm too old for that.
Fair, fat, and forty—that's me!
I look so <u>old</u>.
Fat chance.
I haven't got what it takes.
I have to do twice as much as a man, just to break even.
It's not fair.
I'm so stressed out.
My kids are driving me crazy.
I hate myself!
I can never be good enough.
Why don't I ever get a break?
I'm having a bad day.
I've got PMS.
I can't be bothered.
Just this once won't hurt.
Not again!
I just don't think I'm attractive.
I hate "fat free."
I knew it was too good to be true.
I feel smothered.

I could never learn computers.
I'm afraid to try that.
I'm so embarrassed I could just die!
I wish I were dead.
I wish I'd never been born.
That's the story of my life.
You can't trust anyone anymore.
I'm afraid to get hurt.
He's probably married—all the good ones are.
I can never think of the right thing to say.
I'm such an idiot!
There's <u>no way</u> I'd be caught dead in a swimsuit.
I just <u>look</u> at food and I gain weight.
I've got nothing to wear.
I'm sick and tired of it.
I have a headache.
I need a break.
Two steps forward, one step back.
I'm too skinny.
I give up!
I'll never get a raise.
I don't deserve to win.
I'm too shy.
I'm too outspoken.
I don't like my smile.
How could I <u>do</u> that?
I can never balance my checkbook.
I'd never make it without my coffee.
I'll never see a size 10 again.
I'd lose my head if it wasn't stuck on.
Of <u>course</u> it didn't work.
I don't have a shot!
I'll be late for my own funeral.

I've got two left feet.
I'm an accident waiting to happen.
I just don't have the energy I used to.
I just know I'm going to blow it.
It's just too hard for me.
I don't get it.
I wish it were different.
I wish I were different.
I'm afraid to change.
(. . . and on . . . and on . . . and on.)

And that's just a *brief* sample of the kind of programs we carry around with us every day. It's no *wonder* we have trouble getting where we're going, with that kind of excess baggage in our way!

WHY DOES IT MATTER?

"Okay," you might say, "it's bad enough to know I have those programs, and it's even worse that those old programs cause me to say or think the wrong things about myself. But it's really no big deal, right?"

Wrong.

The problem is that the importance of our programs doesn't stop just with the recording process; that's only the beginning.

So far, we've learned that you get programmed from birth, your programs are actual physical recordings in your brain, and the programs get stronger with repetition. The next key point is critical to understanding the impact the wrong programs can have on every moment of your everyday life.

Key Point #4:
If the strongest program paths you have are built on the wrong program information about you, you will fail, take the wrong action, and continue to send your life in the wrong direction.

Remember, your subconscious mind doesn't know what is true or false about you. Your brain just stores the programs, first a few, then hundreds, and by now, *millions* of programs, and *acts on them as if they were true.*

It is extremely critical what your programs are, because your *programs* end up determining your *behavior.*

Take a moment and consider the importance of that one simple fact: that your *programs* control your *actions.*

YOUR PROGRAMS DETERMINE EVERYTHING ABOUT YOU

Your programs determine everything about you.
It's true. They do.
This doesn't in any way mean that you don't have free will. That came as a gift at your birth, along with some genetic programs like how shy or assertive you are, your basic body type, how quickly you process information, and so on.
Nor does it mean that taking charge of your miraculous

brain takes anything away from your spiritual beliefs or from God's proper direction of your life.

But what's important is that *every area* of your life is affected by the programs you received as you grew up, and by the programs you continue to receive as you live each day of your life.

The following is just a partial list of the things in your life that are affected or controlled by the programs you currently have:

Where you live
The car you drive
Where you go
How you spend your time when you get to choose
The work you do
Your attitude
Whether or not you complain
What you agree to do that you'd rather not do
What you feel guilty about
What you feel good about
Who your friends are, and how many you have
Who your enemies are, and whether you have any
Whether you're married
Who you're married to
Your relationships with your family
Your love relationships
What you want that you don't have
What you're afraid of
What time you get up in the morning
What you eat, or don't eat, and how much
Whether you exercise, and how often
What makes you happy

What makes you angry
Your level of energy
How you feel about yourself every day, in every way

As you can see, the importance of your programs goes far beyond mere words, or a look at the dinner table that told you in no uncertain terms what your mother or father thought about you at that moment, or the way you felt when you did (or didn't) get asked to the prom by the right boy.

We know the programs are there; we know they get recorded, and now we know that everything we do is directed and controlled by the programs we already have.

But how, exactly, does this process work?

Here's what happens.

WHAT DO THOSE "HARMLESS" PROGRAMS *REALLY* DO?

Everything that has ever been said to you, every thought you've ever had, every look of approval and love or disapproval and anger, has been stored in the memory banks of your mind—and *it's all still there.* In order to see how your programs determine your actions, let's take a look into your mental command center.

I like to use the analogy of a big computer control room where the walls are lined floor-to-ceiling with filing cabinets. Think of this as the place where your mind stores its programs.

In this room there is a section of files on Self-Esteem,

one on Health and Fitness, one on Personal Responsibility, one on Relationships, and so on. By the age you are now, each of those file drawers is *full* of the programs you've gotten from yourself and from other people over the years.

Here's an example of the storage process in action.

THE FILING CABINETS AT WORK IN *EVERY* WOMAN'S LIFE

My husband and I were at the grocery store, standing in the checkout line, and a mother with her small son was in line right in front of us. The woman sent her toddler to the bread aisle for a loaf of bread she had forgotten to pick up. When the little boy, who couldn't have been more than 3 or 4 years old, came back proudly carrying the loaf of bread, the mother yelled at him.

"You stupid idiot!" she snapped. "That's *brown* bread, and you should have gotten the *white* bread. Can't you do *anything* right?"

Needless to say, I wanted to take the mother aside and let her know what she had just done to her little boy, but I stopped myself, knowing from painful experience that she would only blame my interference on the child, too, and I would make things worse instead of better. But let's take a look at what happened inside that little boy's mind when he heard his mother's words.

First, the child had successfully carried out his mother's instructions, and was prepared for praise. He had all the file drawers open in his little mind, waiting to record something good about himself. What would his mother say? Would she say how smart he was, how quick, how helpful? Maybe there would even be a reward in the form of a hug, a toy or a treat from the candy aisle.

Instead, the little boy's "reward" was *anger*. When he saw the look on his mother's face, his mental receivers turned to "high," because any strong emotion such as anger creates the strongest chemical impact in the brain.

Whatever his mother said next would create very strong and long-lasting programs that would help tell the little boy about himself in no uncertain terms. And what did he hear, both in the words themselves and in the meaning behind the words?

"You're an idiot. You're stupid. You can't do anything right. I can't trust you. I don't like you. I wish you were different. You make bad choices, and you just ruined my day."

That could sound like an extreme interpretation of a few careless words from the mother, but it's no exaggeration. You've probably heard parents say things like that yourself—and it's an accurate depiction of programming at its worst.

IT HAPPENS TO YOU EVERY DAY

The programming process doesn't stop, either, just because we become adults.

Think about how you feel when someone says something positive to you, for example. Let's say you arrive at work with a slight headache, you've had an argument with your husband before you left the house, your kids are acting up to the point where what the woman in the grocery store said seemed mild in comparison to what you'd like to say to your own children—but as you walk in the door, one of your coworkers sees you come in.

"You look great today!" she says, and you can tell she means it. "New haircut, huh?"

Quick! Run upstairs to your mental computer center and watch the filing process at work.

The first thing you do is dash over to the copy machine on the back wall and make several copies of the new program you just got. You're going to need them, because as you will see, you're going to file that input in more places than one.

WATCH THE PROGRAMMING PROCESS IN ACTION

The drawer on Self-Esteem is already open, from filing the angry words of this morning that your husband didn't mean and will apologize for later. You file a copy of the new message in there, along with all the other messages that help you form the mental picture of who you are.

Across the room is the drawer of files on Appearance—and you've been bombarded for *years* by countless magazine and television ads that have told you what you *should* look like, but probably *don't*. You'd think that file drawer would be too full to hold a single additional program, but there's always room for one more.

You put a copy of your coworker's words in that drawer, too. It slides in right next to the program from when you were twelve years old and your brother said your new haircut looked awful. It didn't, but your mind recorded his words anyway—and believed them.

While you're at it, you notice that the Relationships drawer is still open, from the drive to work when you were thinking about your kids and what kind of mother you are to them. You add a copy of the compliment to the other programs in that drawer about how well you get along with others, and how well they like you.

All this happens in the blink of an eye, before your frown can change to a smile, before you can say, "Thank you."

This same process will repeat itself constantly throughout your day, every day of your life, building and rebuilding your image of who you are, what you can or cannot do, and what you believe will or won't happen to you next.

It wouldn't be so serious if our programs just sat there passively in their file cabinets once we've filed them away. But that's not how it works. When our programs get together in the kind of mass quantity we have as adults, they do something *else*—and that's where the real trouble begins.

WHO'S IN CONTROL
OF YOUR CONTROL CENTER?

To help explain what happens next, I'll use the example of a woman named Melanie. Melanie was up for a raise with her company, and in order to get the raise, she needed to give a computer presentation to the board of directors.

The board meeting was on a Friday. Melanie got up Monday morning and decided she wouldn't wait until late in the week to get started on her presentation. She planned to work on it all evening, and then it would be out of the way.

Melanie got home from work on Monday night at six o'clock, planning to order a pizza so she wouldn't have to cook. When she walked in the door, the first thing she saw was her husband Robert.

Before she could say anything, he gave her a big hug and said, "Surprise, honey, I'm taking you out to dinner tonight. I've already made the reservations . . . how soon can you be ready?"

Freeze-frame Melanie right there, with one hand on the doorknob and a briefcase full of work in her other hand.

WHAT'S REALLY GOING ON?

Run upstairs with me into Melanie's computer control room and watch as program drawers fly open at high speed. One by one, the programs pop up out of the drawers. Over there a program pops up that tells Melanie she has trouble balancing the duties of a wife with the demands of a career. Here's one that says she's really tired, she works too hard, she needs a break . . . and another, that tells her she can work on the presentation later, she's got plenty of time.

A program on fear comes up, the one that's afraid

Robert thinks she's not as attractive as she used to be, and he's spending a lot more time at the office lately. Underneath it all is the program that tells Melanie she might not deserve the raise in the first place . . .

But the programs don't just come up. They're doing something else. One by one, the programs are *voting*, yes or no, *for* Melanie or *against* her future. One by one, the programs are making the decision for her.

It's very simple. Melanie either has more programs in her computer center that tell her she's worth it, that she deserves it, that she can do it—or she has more programs of the other kind, the kind that vote "no."

THE VOTE IS IN

It all happens in an instant. In that split second while Melanie stands still in the doorway, her mouth open to speak, the programs all get together and vote. The results of the vote are printed out on the big monitor screen on the wall right above the copy machine.

The words scroll across the screen, the words that will determine what Melanie does next. The words say,

"Okay to go out to dinner instead of working tonight."

Un-freeze-frame Melanie. She walks in the door, tosses her briefcase on the chair, and says, "I *was* going to work tonight, but just this once, it'll be okay to go out to dinner. I'll work on the presentation tomorrow."

Going out for dinner doesn't sound like a major career mistake, and for most of us it wouldn't have been. But

Melanie's underlying programs that caused that seemingly harmless decision had only begun to do their damage.

On Tuesday, her programs voted again. This time they said she had better take the kids to the soccer game.

By Wednesday, she could feel her energy dropping, and her programs said she should stay in bed all day to avoid a cold (and avoid the presentation looming at the office).

Finally, late Thursday night, after a long day spent catching up from being out of the office on Wednesday, she made a desperate effort to work on the presentation.

Melanie finished working on the presentation at three a.m. on Friday, knowing it was far from her best effort. At work on Friday she looked as tired as she felt.

She gave the presentation a half-hearted effort because she agreed with the little voice in her head that kept reminding her it wasn't very good, and listened with very little surprise to the results: someone else got the promotion, and Melanie didn't. Her negative programs had just reconfirmed themselves.

She thought it was the vote from the board members that cost her the promotion, and the raise that went with it, but Melanie was wrong. It was the vote from her *programs* that destroyed her chances for success—and Melanie *never even knew what had happened.*

YOUR PROGRAMS VOTE—AND YOU WIN OR LOSE

At any given moment, when a question about an action you will take comes up in your mind, the same thing happens: your programs *vote,* "yes" or "no." Your mental computer instantly tallies a total of *all your programs*, and presents you with a decision. The strongest programs always win—and you will act in accordance with the strongest programs you have. The problem is, it happens without your even thinking about it or knowing that it is happening.

Key Point #5:
When you are faced with a conscious or unconscious choice of action, your programs always *vote*.

When that vote takes place, the strongest program pathways you have at that moment will determine what you are thinking, and therefore, what you will do next.

Do you deserve the raise? Will you make that important phone call to the new client? Will you exercise today, and will you feel guilty if you don't? Will you have the skinny salad for lunch, or justify "just one bite" of a rich dessert—again?

Do you argue with your husband, or yell at your children when a little patience would work better? Do you ever promise yourself you will buckle down and finish a project you have started, only to lose momentum halfway through—again?

Are you happy with your level of energy and enthusiasm most of the time, or are you exhausted at the end of the day? Do you promise yourself that you will take some time for *you* this week or this month, only to realize the week or the month is gone and you're last on the list—again?

Most important, do you ever wonder why your life has to be that way?

The answer is, *it doesn't*.

IF YOU CHANGE YOUR PROGRAMS, YOU WILL CHANGE THE RESULTS

The good news is, if you've been losing the vote in the past, there's a way to change your results.

In any situation, you either have more programs that vote for you, or more programs that vote against you. *The key to making your life work better is to change that balance so it will weigh in your favor.*

The reason your programs affect your life so strongly is because when they repeatedly vote on what you should do next, your programs wind up creating your *attitudes* and your *habits*, and your habits and attitudes determine what you do with every minute of every day.

IF YOU WANT TO WIN, YOU HAVE TO CHANGE YOUR PROGRAMS

If you're like most women, there's a very good chance that you have some habits—some *programs*—that you're not entirely happy with.

If you want to win the vote so that your attitudes, your actions, and your habits automatically work for you instead of against you, *you have to change your programs.* But take heart; it can be done, it is not difficult, and it doesn't have to take as long to get new programs as it took you to get the old ones.

Recognizing that you got programmed, that your programs vote for or against you, and that the strongest programs win, are the first and most important steps.

The next step is to learn how to *change* your programs—and in the next few chapters, I'm going to show you exactly how to do that.

If you want to change your programs, then Self-Talk is the answer, because Self-Talk is the most effective way there is to trade your old programs for new ones.

*What could you accomplish,
if you had the <u>right</u> programs
at work in your life
instead of the <u>wrong</u> ones?*

*What can you do,
or dream,
or become,
with the right programs
on your side?*

Chapter 6

HOW TO CHANGE YOUR PROGRAMS

*W*hen you begin to understand the truth about programming, it can be exciting, but it can also seem overwhelming. To think that all of us are victims of the things we are told about ourselves, as well as the programs we receive as a result of everything we experience—to think that we have little or nothing to do with how we turn out, or what we are able to accomplish in life, is a frightening thought.

So far, we've gone over the following key points:
1. We get programmed.
2. The programs are actually physical recordings in the brain.
3. Repeated programs get stronger.
4. If you have the wrong programs, you take the wrong actions.
5. Your programs vote, and the strongest programs win.

It's a good thing the research didn't stop there! Can you imagine the kind of problems we'd be stuck with if we could do nothing to change our programs?

Fortunately, that's not the case. We've learned that there *is* a way to get past the old programs and replace them with new ones. The solution lies in the way we get our programs in the first place.

We learn our habits and behaviors through repetition. The more often we hear something about ourselves, *whether or not it's true to begin with*, the more likely it will become true about us. It's the old story of the self-fulfilling prophecy at work in our lives every day.

It makes sense that if our actions are determined by what we've been told about ourselves, there ought to be a way to change our actions by changing the input we get.

A FOUR-STEP METHOD FOR CHANGING YOUR PROGRAMS

There are four steps involved in the actual process of changing your programs. The four steps are to *monitor*, *edit*, *reprogram*, and *practice*.

1. Monitor

The first step in changing your programs is to *monitor*. That means to listen and pay attention to your old programs. Before you can move forward, you need to get an idea of what your programs already are.

What do you say to others, and to yourself, about you? What do you think you're capable of—or not? What do you most believe to be true about your own ability, talents, skills and potential?

Listen to yourself. Monitor. Pay attention to what your current programs are telling you, so you'll know what areas you want to work on first.

2. Edit

The second step in changing your programs is to *edit*, or change, what you type into your own keyboard. While you're at it, go ahead and modify the kinds of programs you give to others, too. Now that you know your words are much more than a temporary, meaningless expression of how you feel at the moment, do something about it.

Anytime you're about to say the wrong thing, anytime you're in the process of repeating a program that will work against you, *stop*! Stop right in the middle of a sentence, if you have to. Turn it around and say something that will give you, or them, a better program instead. No one will mind. After all, we all know that it's a woman's prerogative to change her mind whenever she feels like it.

Feel free to use that old stereotype to your advantage: change your mind (and your programs) for the better.

3. Reprogram

There are several important ways to change your

programs by changing the input you get. Remember, *repetition* is the key. In order to see positive results, you have to get more program input that works *for* you, and begin to edit out the program input that works *against* you.

We'll cover each of the following steps in greater detail later, but if this page were the only page you read in the book, it could well be the most important. The bottom line is, if you choose to do some of the things I suggest to you next, your programs will change. If you don't, they won't.

You can pick and choose from the menu of choices I've outlined here, but bear in mind that the reprogramming process works best when you use two or more of the methods in combination with each other. Also, the steps are designed to work together in a simple, cohesive way, so my advice is to use all of them.

a. Read and reread the Self-Talk scripts in this book.

Read them out loud, or to yourself. Read them to a friend. Read them to your pet, to your plant, or to your favorite pair of shoes. The more times you get the same repeated input, the better it will work for you.

b. Obtain and listen to professionally recorded cassettes of these word-for-word Self-Talk scripts.

Without a doubt, Self-Talk on tape is the easiest and most effective method to significantly change your programs. If I could recommend only one way for you to work on changing your old programs, this would be the one.

Listening to Self-Talk programs on tape works so well because that's how we got most of our old programs to begin with: by *hearing* them.

I chose to use the tapes myself because I'm very busy, and I wanted to change my old programs in the fastest possible way. It worked for me, in no uncertain terms, and I'm convinced that the same process can help you get where you want to go.

c. Stop accepting *harmful* program input from *any* source.

Your mental computer is the most valuable possession you have. Guard it with your life. It's worth every effort it takes to be sure no one, *ever again*, is allowed to type in anything that will harm you or hold you back in any way.

Your input keyboard is your five senses. Take charge of your keyboard. Protect it. Be careful what you read, and watch, and think, and listen to. Stop letting television and the wrong music and the nightly news and your boss and your negative brother-in-law and people who aren't really your friends steal the best of your future from you! Stop listening to what they say, and start listening instead to the *truth* about you.

If I could encourage you to do one thing differently for the rest of your life, this would be it. If I could help you realize your incredible worth as a human being, your amazing potential for a life well-lived—and then convince you to choose more of the *right* programming from now on—it would be enough to make a real and lasting difference in your life.

Never forget who you are, and what you are. You are a precious, special, and important *woman*. And unfortunately, as a woman, your softness, beauty, and sweetness of spirit is under attack on a daily basis from the world around you. We women, like it or not, have been genetically programmed to be soft and warm and loving and *giving*. But society, especially today, has programmed all too many of us to believe we have to be hard and cold and hateful and *selfish*, in order to survive and succeed.

It's a lie. This misconception isn't true, and never was! I can't speak for you personally, since I don't know the exact circumstances of your life, but I know what works best for me and thousands of women like me:

Be a woman, and don't let anyone tell you that you ought to behave like a man, or act in a way that presents less than the best of you, even for a moment. It harms you in ways you may not even see, and takes away a sense of peace and contentment that I, personally, could find no other way.

As a former soldier, I've lived and excelled in a "man's world." *Been there, done that, maxed it out, and moved on.* And I have to tell you, I like my woman's world a whole lot better. You may find the same to be true for you.

If, on the other hand, you have chosen to enjoy a profession that is traditionally male, you can still be a wonderful, feminine woman. Do your job, and do it better than anyone, and be proud of your achievements! I encourage you to do that, and I applaud your efforts. Just bear in mind as you go through your day that *everything you hear, everything you say,* and *everything you see* will be with you for the rest of your life. Don't sell yourself short; make sure you give yourself only the right input.

   d. Associate with positive and successful people who

give you helpful programs instead of harmful ones.

Now let's examine what happens when you surround yourself with the *right* people, the *real* friends, the *best* input available to you. When you spend time with people who want to help you become your very best self, you naturally exhibit the best of you. You make better choices. You speak more carefully. You make room for dreams in your mind and in your day.

I spend as much time as possible with the kind of people I'd most like to be like. In my business travels, I have been fortunate enough to meet and get to know many fine people. The only problem with that is the word *travel*—because some of my best friends live in cities far from my own home.

It's difficult at times to maintain relationships when I seldom get to see the people I care about, but I make it a point to get together with them whenever I can. I'm willing to work hard at building meaningful friendships with people I can respect and admire, the kind of people who share my sense of principles and values. I don't mind going out of my way to make that happen, because it's so much better being with people who are positive, encouraging, and supportive of my dreams. Being around people like that makes me feel great—and it helps with my *own* self-esteem.

It's worth the time and effort it takes to seek out and spend time with the kind of people who will bring out the best in you. And if you look, you'll find the people who will make a positive difference in your life. Keep in mind that your relationship with them is part of your *programming*—and it's programming that *you* choose.

Spending time with the right people is immensely rewarding, both in the short-term and later on. You already know who those people are, if you are fortunate enough to have them in your life. If not, you can easily figure out where to look, once you decide the right input matters to you.

4. Practice

This is the final step to changing your programs, and it is the most important. Repeated input is the secret to your success. I encourage you to stick with it, keep working at it, and hang in there long enough for the new programs to become a way of life for you. I can say that with enthusiasm, because I know what will happen if you do practice Self-Talk! Believe me, you'll like the results.

After you read the next two sections of programs about who you are and what you do, and you have become familiar with the way your new Self-Talk should sound, you'll be ready to put what you've learned into practice starting immediately.

In Chapter 21, I've given you specific steps and techniques to practice your new Self-Talk. By following those methods, you can easily and naturally add Self-Talk to your everyday life without having to go through anything complicated or time-consuming.

Meanwhile, in the remaining key points about how programming works, I'll show you why *practicing* your new Self-Talk is so important in order to create a *permanent* change in your programs.

USING NEW SELF-TALK
CHANGES YOUR PROGRAMS

Here's how using new Self-Talk will work for you.

When you change your old Self-Talk, you're "typing in" new program messages. Through repetition, the new programs create new pathways in your brain that are clear, straightforward, and strong, and these pathways will lead you in the direction you want to go.

Key Point #6:
Changing your Self-Talk builds new "highways"—(neural pathways)—in the brain by giving you repetition of the *right* program information about you.

Change your Self-Talk. Give yourself the right messages. You're not kidding yourself or pretending to be something you're not; you're just giving your brain a new road map to follow. *You're taking charge.* You're saying, *"This is the way I choose to go, now that I know how it works!"*

Remember, the strongest programs always win when the vote is taken. If you change your programs, you change your actions. You win the vote.

NEW PROGRAMS MEAN NEW *ACTIONS*

By using Self-Talk, you actually create new neural pathways that lead to your success. In the example we used earlier, here's what would have happened if Melanie had decided to change her old programs with Self-Talk. Here's that *same* Melanie *after* she has equipped herself with better programs:

She walks in the door, expecting to work that night, and her husband asks her out to dinner. Freeze-frame Melanie, just like before. Will she take the action that will work for her, or will she follow the old habits? What's going on in Melanie's control center now that she has given herself new programs on self-esteem, finances, and personal organization, among others?

The same file drawers are flying open, the same process is taking place just like before, but things are different now. Melanie has changed the balance of power. Now she can win the vote.

Un-freeze-frame the new Melanie. She walks over to Robert, kisses him on the cheek and says, "Honey, that's very sweet of you, but I have some work to do tonight that's really important to me. If I get started right away, I'll get it done and we'll have the rest of the week free to celebrate—I'm *sure* I'm in the lead for that raise, and this presentation will put me over the top."

This Melanie would have had plenty of time for the soccer game with her kids, and all day Wednesday with Robert, if she still felt like staying home instead of going to work. You see, it all starts with the small, simple step of deciding to change the old programs. Everything else works better after that. It takes the same amount of time, too. You have to be somewhere; *it might as well be somewhere successful.*

GIVE YOURSELF NEW PROGRAMS
AND YOU WILL CHANGE THE OUTCOME

If Melanie *had* chosen to put different programs on her team, she would have had a much better chance of being able to do what it took to get her presentation done on time and in the right way—and the same is true for you. Whatever you've been unable to do, whatever has been stopping you or holding you back in the past, the right programs of Self-Talk can help you overcome those challenges.

If you give yourself strong new Self-Talk programs, they will *outvote* your old negative programs that have been making you less happy or less effective than you want to be, because the strongest programs always win.

Key Point #7:
At the point when your *new* Self-Talk highways are stronger than your old program pathways, you win the vote.

When that happens, you will automatically and naturally take the right action instead of the wrong one. You literally "detour" around the old program roads that have been getting in the way of your momentum and forward progress. You take the new highway instead.

Your old programs may have been built haphazardly, and if they are strong, they're strong *by accident.* Your new Self-Talk programs will be built by *design,* so they get stronger, *faster*—and they will help you win *on purpose.*

The most exciting part, the breakthrough that the neuroscientists are able to show us with the latest computer technology, is the next key point. If you understand this single, incredibly important fact, you'll know more about who you are, why you do what you do, and what to do about it than most people will ever know.

Key Point #8:
When you stop using the old neural pathways *long enough*, and use the new Self-Talk highways instead, the *old* program highways will break down, because you're not feeding them anymore.

That's the secret. *That's the breakthrough.* That's why Self-Talk works!
The old program paths break down.
They break down. They go away. They lose their strength and their control over you and the direction of your life. If you stay with it long enough, if you get off the old highways *by using the new ones instead*, you *physically change* the chemical pathways of your brain.
Your road map will be different.
When you change your programs, not only will you be driving on the new highways, it will get harder and harder to use the old ones, even if you wanted to, because they will not be in working order anymore! Your brain isn't stupid. It uses the strongest pathways available to it—and your job is simply to determine for yourself which pathways those are.

HOW LONG DOES IT TAKE?

How long does it take to start to break down an old

program path when you're not using it anymore? It's a fascinating answer.

We've all heard the expression, "It takes 21 days to change a habit." We didn't know it at the time, but it is completely chemical. Your habits are nothing more than programs that are so strong you can follow them without thinking about it. And it takes a minimum of about *three weeks* for the old program pathways to begin to lose their physical nutrition and even *begin* to break down.

That doesn't mean that in three weeks' time, all your troubles will go away. What it *does* mean, however, is that in a short time, you will begin to see results. And those results build success upon success, one small step after another, so that before you know it, you look back on your life and see a definite difference.

In case you're wondering, age has very little to do with it. The old saying about not being able to teach an old dog new tricks is false. Whether you're eight or eighty (or "29 and holding"), you can benefit from using new Self-Talk. As long as your brain is healthy and functioning, you *can* build new program paths. Self-Talk techniques have even been found to be helpful in some cases of clinical depression and stroke recovery.

Your brain was designed to continue the process of getting new programs until the day you die. If you follow the steps to reprogram, your brain has no choice but to change. It's never too early to build new highways, and it's never too late.

YOU START TO WIN
WHEN YOU KNOW HOW IT WORKS

Think back to my earlier question about whether you have some programs, or habits, you'd like to change. There is a way, and now you know how it works:

You get programmed. The programs are physically, chemically there in the brain; they're real. When you repeat them, the programs get stronger. If you have the wrong programs, you lose, because your programs vote and the strongest ones win.

Changing your Self-Talk changes your programs through repetition. When the Self-Talk highways—the new pathways that you create with the new Self-Talk—are stronger than your old programs, you win the vote. Your old program paths then begin to break down and lose their strength, because you're not using them and they aren't being fed anymore.

The changes *start* there, but the best is yet to come.

WHAT HAPPENS WHEN THE NEW SELF-TALK TAKES OVER

All of those earlier key points are important, when it comes to understanding how Self-Talk works. But it gets really exciting when you get to these final two points, because this is when the new Self-Talk begins to take off on its own.

Key Point #9:
In time, with repetition, the new Self-Talk program pathways are so strong that they have formed a new set of habits, a new set of attitudes, and a new set of beliefs

about yourself—so you take the *right* path *without having to think about it.*

The more you use your new Self-Talk, the more new programs you build, the better it will work for you, because that's when your automatic *habits* will change.

To me, this is very important. It's what we do *when we're not consciously thinking about it* that counts the most. Most of us can take temporary control over our current situation if we make up our minds to do so—but we women are short on time and long on stress. I don't know about you, but I don't have time to be constantly worrying about whether I'm doing the right things at the right time and in the right order.

I only have time for "autopilot." I know how powerful habits can be, so I've worked to program myself to take more of the right actions without having to think about it. My life is much easier now, because I changed my programs.

Self-Talk has helped me do better in many ways, but the following illustration will show you one powerful way that my new programs added more positive moments to my life than I ever thought possible.

THE RIGHT SELF-TALK
CAN CHANGE YOUR DAY

I used to be grumpy in the mornings. I've always been more of a "night" person who likes to stay up late. I love to sleep, and especially to sleep *late*. No matter what time it was when I woke up, the process of getting out of bed was a slow and often unpleasant one.

With the right Self-Talk programs in place, I can finally appreciate mornings in a way that used to be impossible for me. I won't pretend I no longer like sleeping in, because I do. But the *process* of getting up is different for me now.

Because I changed my programs about waking up, it's nearly impossible for me to get up in the morning and say, "*It's going to be another one of those days.*"

Do I have to *think* about whether I feel positive and energetic when I wake up? No. The programs are just there, running my computer control center, voting exactly the way my brain was designed to do. The difference is that I have built habits and attitudes that work *for* me instead of *against* me.

I still like to stay up late, but mornings are no longer the ordeal they used to be. Imagine the difference between a groan and a smile, first thing in the morning! And all those little moments add up.

The right Self-Talk changed my life day by day. When my morning starts off by getting up on the right side of the bed instead of the wrong one, everything works better. I'm happier, my husband *really* appreciates my new attitude, and I've even managed to add the beauty of seeing a sunrise now and then.

WHY SELF-TALK HELPS YOU MAKE CHANGES THAT *LAST*

Once you have the new program pathways in place, the final long-term benefit of Self-Talk begins to happen.

This is a process that, *on its own*, will continue to add positive benefit for the rest of your life.

Here's how Self-Talk helps you create *lasting* changes.

Key Point #10:
Once your new Self-Talk program pathways are in place, the strongest programs you have will *automatically* attract new input that agrees with what is already there.

When you have enough new programs, they begin to build themselves *on their own*.

Your strongest programs bring their friends.

It's up to you which programs will be in charge of you and which will bring more programs like them home to stay.

I hope you understand how important this single idea is to your future. To me, it's an amazing thought to realize that your brain, *all by itself*, makes more of the kind of programs it has most.

With your new Self-Talk programs firmly in charge, you'll no longer have to think about the process. Your brain will automatically begin to hear the more *positive* program messages directed at you and act on *those*—and make *them* come true.

YOU DECIDE
WHICH SIDE WINS

The negative programs will still be all around you, but you won't respond to them in the same way, because your brain is building on its strongest highways, and those are highways that go in your direction! It's incredibly exciting to realize the true impact of what happens when you *automatically and naturally* attract positive programs.

At that point, you can literally decide to do *anything* you want to do and go in *any direction* you choose to go, because you are finally in control of your programs and your life.

A LOOK BACK,
AND THE NEXT STEP FORWARD

By now, you should have a clear understanding of programming and how it works. Let's look at those key points we've covered, so they will be firmly fixed in your mind.

o You get programmed. We all do.
o The programs are chemical, physical pathways in the brain.
o The more you repeat a program, the stronger it gets.
o Your programs direct your actions; what you do is determined by the programs you have.
o Throughout each day, every day of your life, your programs constantly vote—for you or against you—and the strongest programs win.
o If you use the right Self-Talk in the right way, you can change your programs.
o When your new programs are stronger than the old ones, you win the vote, and your actions will change

in your favor.

o   When you repeat a program, you feed it and make it stronger. If you get off the old programs, and stop feeding them, they weaken and break down.

o   Your new programs eventually create a new set of attitudes, habits and "truths" about you that you follow naturally.

o   The process continues on its own, in a positive ongoing cycle, with the strong new programs automatically building more programs like them.

What if it's true?
It is.
What if you *do* get programmed?
You do.
What if your programs literally determine your success or failure, decide whether you reach your goals or not, and help to chart your ultimate direction in life?
They do.
And what if there's finally something you can do about it?
There is.
If you want to take control of your programs, this next part is where it begins—because this is where it gets personal. This next section is all about *you.*

Part II
YOUR PROGRAMS
ABOUT WHO YOU ARE

*Imagine for a moment
what your very best self
would be,
if you could design her
and make her a reality.*

*What would that
"new and improved"
woman, <u>you</u>,
be like?*

Chapter 7

CREATING YOUR VERY BEST SELF

*I*f you could choose the qualities you would most like to create in yourself, what would that "new and improved" woman—*you*—be like?

Would you be more relaxed? Would you be more goal-directed, or a person who achieves more? Would you be a happier woman, who gets along well with others and makes friends easily? A better mother? More organized? Would you have more money in the bank, or would you be "retired" from your current job and spend more time with your family?

Where would you live? What kind of car would you drive? Would you travel more—or stay home more? Would you be more assertive, or do you hope you'd speak your mind a little less often than you do right now?

What would your relationships be like? Would you take vacations, and if so, where would you go and what would you do when you got there? Would you give yourself the luxury of time alone when you needed it, or would you rather fill your life with newfound or rediscovered friends? What would you do with your time, if you got to choose? Most important, *will* you get to choose?

When you read the Self-Talk scripts in the following chapters, imagine that you're reading from a menu of choices, except this time, the menu is all about you, and the restaurant is your life. I'm not suggesting that you will suddenly undergo a miraculous transformation in every area of your life at once—but over time, Self-Talk, properly applied, *does* make a tremendous difference in more ways than you think.

WHAT DO YOU WANT SELF-TALK TO DO FOR YOU?

Imagine typing the right programs into your own computer. What could you accomplish, if you had the right programs at work in your life instead of the wrong ones—and how would you feel? What can you do, or dream, or become, with the right programs on your side?

Remember, anything worthwhile takes time and effort, and there are no shortcuts. Any lasting change takes at least 21 days. But using Self-Talk has a way of helping you make subtle changes in the way you live your life each day. You'll notice small improvements *immediately*, and there's an opportunity for major positive results in the long run.

If you stick with it, and add a good healthy dose of

84

goal-setting along with the right Self-Talk, chances are you will become much more like that "ideal" version of you we've been talking about. You *can* decide to work at creating the person *you* choose to be instead of the person who was mapped out for you by the opinions and expectations of everyone *else* around you.

Sounds like fun, doesn't it? I hope by now you can't wait to meet that wonderful "new" self, the woman who lives inside you and hardly ever gets to *be herself*. I hope you're ready to get started, and that you're looking forward to meeting her right away. I know I am, and I probably don't even know you yet!

It starts with *you*, and the changes you want to make for yourself—and if that's all Self-Talk did for you, it would be enough. But it doesn't *end* with you, because the way *you* are has an impact on everyone *around* you. What happens next is exciting, because what happens next is that *your* new programs begin to positively affect the *other* people in your life that you care about most.

WHAT KIND OF DIFFERENCE CAN THE RIGHT PROGRAMS MAKE?

Imagine the power of learning how to give the *right* programs to your kids, your husband and the other people in your life! What can you do for them, knowing that programs can change, and people can change too?

Think what it would be like to be around people who had decided to change their programs for the better. What would your home be like? What kind of changes would your family make?

I know what it's like, because I live in a home like that—and it's a different kind of place entirely. It's better.

I'm not saying we're perfect people, or that Self-Talk will make all your problems disappear. But once you're *aware* of the process, it does change your life *minute by minute*, and then those minutes become hours and days and then months and eventually years of a happier, more peaceful, and more productive existence. The little changes add up to changing your life.

Think about where you work, if you have a traditional job. How different would your day be, if that one co-worker who drives you nuts would somehow lose her negative attitude and stop complaining all the time? What if it could get even a little better?

It's not her *fault*. It's her *programs*—and it doesn't have to stay that way. Try typing in some new programs to her mental computer. She might not listen at first, and she may wonder what on earth has gotten into you, but I've seen it work many times. You can help her, and help everyone else's day in the process. Try it. You've got nothing to lose but a headache.

WHAT KINDS OF PROGRAMS ARE YOU TYPING IN?

It's all too easy to remember the negative or disbelieving remarks we heard growing up—and still hear all too often today. But how many times can you recall being told how *good* you were, what you *could* do, what you did *right* instead of wrong? Many times? A handful? *Or none at all?*

The people who programmed us—our parents, our siblings, our teachers and our friends—were doing their best, but *they didn't know what they were doing* when it came to giving others the right programs. They didn't know how it worked—but now, *you do.*

Knowing this, you have a responsibility to be careful about the words that come out of your mouth. They're *not* harmless. They can hurt. The good news is, if you get it right, they can also help.

Once you know how programming works, along with the responsibility for doing it right comes an amazing opportunity to help the people you care about.

Anytime you tell another person *anything*, especially if you're talking to a child or a young person, remember this: *You're typing programs into that person's mental keyboard*—and what you say, if repeated often enough, will be acted on as if it's *true.*

Knowing that, what will you type?

IT'S TIME TO GET
SOME NEW PROGRAMS

In the next section of the book we're going to focus on the twelve main areas of a woman's life. In the following chapters, I've given you new Self-Talk scripts—new programs that can help you have more of what you want, in each of the areas we're covering.

If you're not yet sure exactly what you want Self-Talk to do for you, but you know you're a woman who wants to make some changes, I recommend that you pay particular attention to the chapter on setting goals. By the time you finish that area of Self-Talk, you should have a much clearer picture of who you are and what you want from your life.

Now let's apply the new Self-Talk to your daily life. It's time to get some new programs.

I'll begin with that most important (and most often misunderstood) area of all—the area of programs that have to do with your *self-esteem*.

The ultimate difference
between those women
who can do anything,
and those
who do nothing,
is their <u>belief</u>
in themselves.

Chapter 8

SELF-TALK FOR SELF-ESTEEM

*T*he subject of self-esteem is probably the most talked about, and the most *misunderstood*, component of personal growth. These days, we are constantly assaulted from all sides with the voices that tell us if we don't build positive self-esteem, we don't have a shot. We hear it from educators, from congressmen, from therapists, from members of the clergy, from our kids and even from the guy on the evening news.

But what does it *mean*, this confusing and difficult requirement of having good self-esteem? And how, exactly, are we supposed to go about getting it, for ourselves, for our children and for the other people we care about?

The answer begins in understanding what self-esteem really is, and what it *isn't*.

WHAT SELF-ESTEEM IS NOT

In order to understand what self-esteem is, let's start by taking a look at what self-esteem *is not*.

Self-esteem does *not* mean "liking yourself." That's the definition most people would choose, but it's not accurate.

Building your self-esteem with Self-Talk will *help* you like yourself more, and even help you learn to love yourself with all your faults and failings, because the right self-esteem can help you see beyond your limitations to the strengths and talents and skills you have within you. But self-esteem and self-love are two different things.

Another popular misconception is that having high self-esteem means you're conceited, or "full of yourself." There is a major difference between confidence and conceit. When you meet people who act like they are conceited or arrogant, they are almost always suffering from *low* self-esteem.

Another common mistake people make is to assume that self-esteem is bad, or sinful. The reality is that the process of building strong, healthy self-esteem *doesn't* mean you're trying to take something away from God, or that you are no longer humble in an appropriate way.

WHAT IS SELF-ESTEEM, *REALLY?*

Self-esteem actually has a very precise meaning. The word "esteem" comes from the word "estimation." Self-esteem is your *estimation* of yourself—your *assessment* of who you think you are.

Self-esteem is your appraisal of yourself.

What do you think of you? What do you sincerely believe you are capable of accomplishing? What do you feel your limitations are? What kind of person do you see yourself to be, and what impression of yourself do you present to others?

How do you act in each and every situation? How do you feel? How do you respond to the people and circumstances of your life?

Your self-esteem is *everything* you believe about *you.*

Who are you, *in your own opinion*, and what do you think you can do?

WHAT CAN YOU DO TO BUILD STRONGER SELF-ESTEEM?

If your picture of yourself is not as favorable as you would like it to be, there are some things you can do to change that picture.

You're doing better than you think you are. If you're like most of us, you're probably being much too quick to focus on your shortcomings and too hesitant to acknowledge your strengths. I know without a doubt that if I could spend even a few minutes with you, I could show you a newer and better snapshot of who you are and what you are capable of.

If we were to sit down over a cup of coffee and have a conversation, in your kitchen or in mine, I guarantee you

I could identify many good points about you that you may be unaware of. Anyone who knows you could do the same.

If you wonder whether this is true, just think of anyone *you* know. You can, and do, see good things about other people every day. You may even already be in the habit of pointing them out to people, by giving them sincere compliments when you notice something they're doing well.

The key, then, lies in finding a way to get you to see the good things about *yourself* that others see more easily than you do. It's not false praise to tell you that you have talents and skills and abilities that you may not even be aware you have. It's the truth.

The solution to building better self-esteem is simple. If you want to change your image of who you are, you have to build new program highways that paint that picture for you. You have to change your programs *about yourself* and begin to see yourself in a whole new light.

You already have within you the ability to succeed at anything you try. The ultimate difference between those women who can do anything and those who do nothing is *belief*. It sounds simple to say "you can if you think you can," but when you look at it from the standpoint of *programming* that belief, it makes a lot more sense.

If you want to have better self-esteem, you have to *program* it in.

GIVING YOURSELF NEW PROGRAMS
OF SELF-ESTEEM

The following script of Self-Talk will help you build stronger and more positive self-esteem. The more you program in these phrases, and others like them, the easier it will be for you to believe in yourself.

We'll get to specific techniques later on that will show you the best ways to use Self-Talk to change your old programs and build new ones. For now, as you read the new program phrases you see here, all you need to do is mentally picture what it would be like to *be* the kind of person with strong, healthy programs like these.

Self-Talk for Self-Esteem

I believe in myself. I focus on creating the best possible picture of myself in my mind, and I work hard to be that person in my life.

Whenever a question comes up that says, "Can I do this? Am I good enough? Will I make it?" an immediate answer comes to my mind that says, "Yes, I can . . . yes, I am . . . yes, I will!"

I keep my mind focused on the highest attributes of character, personal responsibility, trustworthiness, dignity, and honor. My goals keep me on the right path, and I concentrate on progressing toward a worthwhile future.

I never compromise my integrity for a short-term solution. Instead, I find a way to make my life work for the greater good, by setting my sights on a positive long-term perspective.

I am a quality person, and it shows in everything I say and do.

Other people notice me because of the way I choose to conduct myself. I keep high standards, not only because they are watching me, but because I am.

I am consistent in my words, my thoughts and my actions in all things. I can be trusted to do what I say I will do, to the absolute best of my ability.

I keep going when other people stop, falter, or fall back. I am strong, confident, in control, and happy to be who I am.

There is no challenge that can defeat me. I was created to be my very best, and I tackle every problem in my life with an attitude that assumes success will be the outcome.

Every day, I work at being better, in a modest, healthy way. And as I go, I grow.

If there is ever a time when I doubt myself, I look behind me at the victories of my past, and I look forward to the fulfillment of my potential. Then I focus on faith, and take action.

I don't dwell on my own shortcomings. I keep a true heart and a solid dream in front of me at all times.

Whenever I am faced with a negative attitude toward the person I choose to be, I simply remind myself that they don't know me well enough yet to understand who I am. Then I let it go.

When someone I respect tells me what I'm doing wrong, I take it to mind and work to correct my behavior—but I never take it to heart in a way that will hurt me. I take the good, leave the bad, and get on with my life.

I believe in a bright future. I am cheerful and optimistic, and other people like to be around me.

I replace doubt with decision, anger with a loving attitude, fear with a focus on the future, and hesitation with hope.

I make it a point each day to leave the world a better place because I was there.

Every day my belief grows stronger, my sights are set higher, and my goals are nearer to my reach.

I enjoy the life I am creating for myself, because of the belief in my heart that I am worth the effort it takes to make it happen.

First, I make sure my dreams represent the kind of person I would most like to be, and then I work to live my dreams.

I approach every new day with a thankful attitude, for the chance to become the person I was born to be. I like myself, I love my life, and I am happy to be who I am!

Imagine what your life would be like if you really believed those kinds of things about yourself! When you put the right programs of Self-Talk to work for you, using the techniques I'll explain to you shortly, those words and others like them will become true about you.

That's not a myth, or a fantasy. Those words and ideas might seem unrealistic or completely untrue about you right now, but that doesn't matter. Program them in anyway. Repeat them and repeat them and repeat them until you begin to recognize they *do* apply to you, that they *do* paint a picture of who you really are.

The goal of all Self-Talk is to show you the truth about you, to introduce you to the very best self you are capable of creating and living out each day. To begin with, the changes in your beliefs about yourself will be subtle and small, but those moments add up.

The voting process we talked about earlier is constant, and the daily challenges and questions you face may not change. The difference will be in *you*. It's like balancing two sides of a scale. The moment you have more programs that give you a picture of yourself as a strong, healthy, capable, effective, contented person, the scale tips the right way, and *the vote will go in your favor*.

AN EXAMPLE OF
POSITIVE SELF-ESTEEM IN ACTION

To illustrate my point, let's take another look at my friend who overcame bulimia and went on to become a happy, healthy woman. "Fatty Patty" became a thing of the past for her, and she never went back.

She won that battle by a determined, nonstop effort of programming in a completely different picture of herself. Surprisingly to some, her problem wasn't in her mental files on weight or health or appearance. The issue with her was self-esteem.

Starting with her parents, then the kids at school, and eventually with the programs she repeated to herself, my friend had formed a *false* self-image that told her she was fat and destined to stay that way. She believed people didn't like her or see her as a valuable and worthwhile person, and she had difficulty living up to her expectations of who she thought they wanted her to be.

Her impression of herself was *inaccurate*. She got robbed of precious years of happiness by programs that weren't even true about her! In her natural state, my friend is a healthy, normal-sized woman who doesn't have a weight problem, and never will again.

She got past her past, and here's how she did it:

a. She put people in her life who would tell her the *right* truths about who she was, instead of contributing to the old, *false* picture that had harmed her.

b. She began to edit out *all* negative input, and began to build new program highways to her healthy future.

c. She decided to get the Self-Talk tapes and listen to them. The Self-Talk scripts on tape gave her the positive daily repetition and reinforcement she needed to start breaking down her old mental program pathways of self-doubt and disbelief.

d. She gave herself a new nickname, so every time the old thought came up that reminded her of what didn't work, she had something to replace it with.

Through Self-Talk and reprogramming, my friend showed herself a *new* self-esteem picture of who and what she really was.

Did it take time? Yes, it did, but she would have been another week or month or year older anyway, and she would still have still been stuck with the same old programs if she hadn't taken the time to change them.

Did it take effort? It was much easier than she had thought it would be. The reprogramming process took nowhere near as much work or time as she thought it would, especially considering that it made such a critical difference in her life.

Did the changes last? Absolutely.

As it turned out, my friend discovered she is a wonderful and warm person who is very easy to like. She is a much happier person, she gets along well with others, and she looks *great*—especially when she smiles, which she does a lot more often these days.

WHAT IF YOU'VE BEEN SEEING A FALSE PICTURE OF YOU?

You may not believe it yet, but I'm here to tell you that if you think you're no good, if you think someone else can achieve but you can't, if you think it's harder for you than for someone else, if you think you can't change and you're stuck with the same old "you" that's been making you unhappy and holding you back all these years— *you're wrong*.

There *is* something you can do about it. You *can* take one small but vital step in the right direction. All you have to do is decide to change your programs of self-esteem, and the rest will get better on its own.

SELF-TALK WORKS
WHETHER YOU BELIEVE IT OR NOT

For now, don't worry about *believing* the new messages you're hearing about yourself. It doesn't matter if you believe the new programs yet; in fact, if you believed all the Self-Talk you just read at the beginning of this chapter, we probably wouldn't be having this conversation. You would already have the kind of strong self-esteem you need to help you reach your goals.

Your home computer doesn't have to believe the words you type into it in order to perform the new instructions; it simply acts on the programs it gets. Your subconscious mind works the same way; the new programs are effective—*whether you believe them at first, or not*.

If men and women
were the same,
men would buy more shoes.

Chapter 9

SELF-TALK FOR POSITIVE RELATIONSHIPS

*W*hoever said, "no man is an island," should have said it about a woman. I've observed many men that I'm convinced would be quite happy if left alone, thank you very much, but I've never yet met a woman who would.

As women, we are defined in large part by the people with whom we have chosen to share our lives. The structure of our relationships defines the structure of our lives, in a much stronger way than it does for a man.

We play different roles and call on different program areas for being a daughter than we do for being a mother, for example. Our role as a wife is different from our role as a professional supervisor (regardless of whether our husbands believe the truth of that statement). We have other programmed roles for being a worker, a lover, a friend, a sister, a nurturer, a leader, a supporter, and a teacher, to name just a few.

Men, on the other hand, are generally called upon to present pretty much the same personality whether they are at work, at play, at home, or somewhere in between. They act in a similar, guy-like way whether they are with their fathers, their sons, their wives, their golf buddies or their bosses.

I'm generalizing, of course, and I know better than to imply all men are alike. There are differences in their behavior, of course, but the *range* of roles for men is much more limited than it is for us women. Men can even wear the same clothes and shoes in all those places, with all those different people, and no one thinks a thing about it!

THERE *IS* A DIFFERENCE

If you want to recognize the truth of the many roles women play in comparison to those for men, take a look at the shoe shelf in the average *woman's* closet.

We have shoes that we wear to work, to let our boss and our coworkers know how professional we are. We have athletic shoes that we wear when we go walking with the other women on our block, and more athletic shoes that we buy so we won't feel so guilty about not exercising as often as we should.

We have dressy shoes that our husbands *think* are for their benefit, but all women know we put those on to impress the *other* women in the restaurant or at the party, and prove we dress as well as they do. The husband thing is just a plus.

We have shoes to wear when we're relaxing with our friends, and shoes to wear to mow the yard in when our teenaged kids say they will and haven't yet, and shoes to wear to the beach with the baby and shoes to wear when we're meeting our best friend to go out shopping for—what else?—more shoes.

Most men, on the other hand, can get by with three basic pairs of shoes: dress shoes, casual or athletic shoes, and one pair we women call the "I-can't-*believe*-you're-going-to-bring-those-things-inside-this-house" shoes.

It's a fact.

WHY A WOMAN WOULD CLIMB A MOUNTAIN

You've probably heard about the man who was asked why he decided to climb Mount Everest. He said, in a strong and manly few words, *"Because it is there."*

His answer had to do with him, and the mountain, and very little else.

But what would happen if you asked a *woman* the same question? For starters, the answer would take a *lot* more words—and it would involve more people.

Here is *my* list of potential answers to the question of why an average woman might decide to climb a mountain:

"Because I need to lose those extra ten pounds."
"Because my brother did it."

"Because I <u>said</u> I would, and I'd be too embarrassed to back down now."
"Because the guys at work said I'd never make it."
"Because my friends are all going."
"Because it could be a <u>great</u> place to meet a new man!"
"Because my dad wanted a boy, and got me instead."
"Because I <u>want</u> to, okay?"
"Because it takes special shoes, so I'll have to go shopping."
. . . etc., etc., etc.

My mountain-climber woman would *still* be talking as she went out of sight over the hill—and people say men and women are no different!

THE WOMAN
WHO CLIMBED MOUNT EVEREST

Before you begin to think I'm reinforcing an old, negative stereotype of women as weak in body or mind, let me reassure you. I'm kidding.

But that humorous example *does* bring up a good point about how women are perceived, and how easy it is to put ourselves down.

It's wonderful to see the kind of positive role models for women who help reframe those old beliefs about what women can do. I watched a recent interview featuring a woman like that, and I'd like to share it with you.

The woman, along with 31 other climbers, made it to within a few hundred meters of the top of Mount

Everest. The group reached the turn-around point, the specific moment when they had spent the maximum safe amount of time on the mountain. To continue in spite of the reduced oxygen in the atmosphere would mean that some, if not all, of the mountaineers would almost certainly die. They had no choice but to turn around and go back down the mountain.

When asked how it felt to be so close to the summit and have to turn around, the woman didn't focus on how close she had come to the top without making it, nor did she see the climb as a failure. She mentioned how important it was that all the climbers were safe, in spite of the odds to the contrary. Then she said something that made a real impact on me.

"I was standing almost at the summit of the mountain," she said, "and the whole world was spread out before me. It came to me in that moment that in the Tibetan language, the name for Mount Everest means "the place of the female eagle. It was worth the climb."

The place of the *female* eagle. Think about it.

A STRONG WOMAN'S REASONS
FOR CLIMBING THE MOUNTAIN

I've mentioned a man's reason for climbing the mountain, and included a fun list of reasons why the "typical" woman might do the same thing.

But there's really no such thing as a "typical" woman—and it wouldn't be right to end this section without including what a woman with strong, healthy programs might say if she was asked that question:

"Because I believe in myself."
"Because I am strong."
"Because I won't quit."
"Because I set goals, and I do what it takes to reach them."
"Because I belong at the top."
"Because I can!"

WHY I CLIMBED MY OWN "MOUNTAIN"

When people learn that I am a former US Army Soldier of the Year, they almost always ask two questions.
"Why did you join the Army?" and
"How and why did you become Soldier of the Year?"
My answers to both of those questions are significantly different than they would be for a man, because my answers have to do with more than personal achievement. My reasons had as much to do with the other *people* in my life at the time as they did with my own goals.

By midway through my sophomore year of college, I had run out of money. I was working two jobs, and I was still broke. I decided to enter the military because of their college program. But why the Army?

My mother's brother fought in the Army during World War II. My father was in the Army during the Korean War, and his brother was a bomber pilot in the Army Air Corps. My sister's husband was in the Army during the Vietnam War.

I chose the military because of my future; I chose the Army because of my *family*.

In part, the same holds true for why I would attempt the near-impossible task of becoming Soldier of the Year.

I was stationed in Germany in the 3rd Infantry Division, the most decorated division in the history of the Army. I was in a unit made up mostly of men, although the respect level for the female soldiers was very high. The morale among my fellow soldiers was strong. We were a *team*, partly because we were Americans far from home in a foreign country, and partly because we knew we were doing an important job.

When my company commander recommended that I enter the competition, beginning with Soldier of the Month, then of the Quarter, and ending with Soldier of the Year, I didn't want to let him down. I wanted to do my best to represent my friends and teammates. I wanted to know I could do it for my *own* reasons of personal satisfaction and sense of self, of course. But I was *also* motivated to succeed because of the *people* I cared about most.

I wanted to make my parents proud of me.

I wanted to prove that a woman could do it.

I wanted to meet the best male soldiers on their own terms, and win not *because* I was female but *in spite* of it.

I GAVE IT MY BEST

Over the next several months, I got the chance to prove myself, and then some. To win each level of the competition, I had to excel in all areas of military life: physical fitness and endurance, ability with weapons ranging from a 45 pistol and an M16 rifle to machine guns and grenade launchers, first aid techniques, military history, and leadership. I had to prove that I knew how to defend myself in case of a nuclear, chemical, or biological attack.

For the final competition, I had to face a panel of eight Sergeants-Major with a combined military experience of more than two hundred years among them. All eight of them fired questions at me at high speed, and it was my task to answer each and every question without making a mistake or losing my composure.

When I became Soldier of the Year for the 3rd Infantry Division of the US Army in Europe, they honored me with a parade in Stuttgart in which all the units represented in the competition marched past me in full military splendor.

It was worth all the pain, exhaustion, drills, weapons practice, mud, sweat, and tears it took to win, just to see the looks on the faces of my platoon members that day. Their salutes meant that I had succeeded, that I had done what I had set out to do. I had made them proud of me, and I had reached my goal.

FOR WOMEN,
IT'S ALL CONNECTED

It is impossible to separate "who we are" from who we are in relationship to the other people in our lives. It all overlaps, especially for women. We define ourselves daily and rate how well our lives are going by how "good" we are at dealing with our husbands and our fathers, our sisters and our brothers, our mothers, our lovers, our coworkers, our bosses, all other women, our friends, and even our enemies.

For women, almost everything in life is directly or indirectly related to the subject of relationships. For instance, if you want to lose a few pounds (or a few more than that), it *might* have to do with your desire to be fit and healthy—but I'd be surprised if a personal relationship (or a desire for a personal relationship) weren't involved in there somewhere, too.

How you feel about the amount of money you'd like to make has only partly to do with whether you can pay the bills on time. It's also connected with the *people* you associate with—your business relationships, your friendships, and how you want people to perceive the way you handle your finances. Your money programs can even be affected by what level of people you want to be able to afford to be with socially, or which school you want to be able to afford for your children.

Personal organization issues aren't limited to a desire to be on time and to have an empty "to-do" list or an empty "in" basket at the end of the day. Often, your urge to do better in this area is really about how well-respected you are as a competent person, sometimes by your own standards but all too often by the standards of the people around you.

The same holds true for almost any area of self-improvement we feel the urge to undertake: our desire to excel has at least as much to do with how we relate to others as it has to do with the "real" subject at hand.

RELATIONSHIPS CREATE STRONG PROGRAMS

Many of our strongest programs are the ones associated with the people with whom we share our lives.

No one can make me feel better than one of the people I love, and no one can make me feel worse with a chance remark than one of those same people. When you care about maintaining a relationship with another person, every word counts. Everything that other person says and does assumes a stronger and more important meaning than if a stranger said or did the same thing.

The programs you got from your parents set your early patterns about how your relationships would go. I won't go deeply into that subject, since we're not here for therapy and there are countless books on the subject of the relationship you had or now have with your mother and father. I mention it now only so you will be aware of where your style of setting up and maintaining relationships came from.

Some of us were lucky. I got plenty of hugs and kisses as a child, and got told often that I was loved.

My family was affectionate, and so is my own basic personality, but I also needed to add new programs to build on what was already working for me. With the right programs in place, I'm never intimidated at the thought of meeting new people. I naturally assume the best about the people I meet, because my primary program superhighway about interacting with other people tells me to do that.

But what if the programs you got about forming and keeping good relationships were less than the best? What kind of problems have been caused in your life, what kind

111

of hurt and loneliness have you been forced to put up with, simply because when the right relationship programs were passed out, you got left out of the loop?

I want to reassure you that if you don't yet have the kind of relationships in your life that you'd like to have, there's something you can do about it. It's a powerful thing to realize that no matter how bad your old programs are in this area, you don't have to keep missing out.

HOW WELL DO YOUR RELATIONSHIPS WORK FOR YOU?

How *are* you at dealing with other people? Do you see yourself as someone who gets along well with everyone, or does your life seem to be a constant series of battles?

Are you happy and fulfilled in a romantic and loving relationship, or is your "significant other" a TV remote control?

Would you like to find a new romantic relationship, or improve your current love life? Would you like to relate better with the people at work and make new friends without being afraid of not doing something right?

The following script of Self-Talk will show you the way. As you read, think of building strong new program pathways in your brain, the roads that lead to a future filled with positive relationships.

Self-Talk for Positive Relationships

People like me, and I like them.

In any relationship I have, I always give my best. I give my time, my belief, my love, and my energy.

I never dwell on the negative qualities of the people in my life. I look for the best in everyone I meet.

In any conversation, I pay attention to what is really being said. I'm a good listener, and people find it easy to talk to me.

I expect the best from myself and from others—and that's what I get.

I really enjoy spending time with my friends. I always make time for them, and they are there for me, too.

I seek out and find people who share my values, encourage my goals, and believe in me. And I do the same for them.

If there is a problem in my relationship with someone, I never ignore it or avoid it. I take the time to talk it through, work it out, and move forward in a positive direction.

My life is richer because I share it with others.

When I love someone, I let them know it. When I like someone, it shows!

113

I take personal responsibility in everything I do. People can count on me, because they know I am a person they can trust.

When someone really needs me, I always try to help. And I smile when I tell them, "Yes!"

I choose to build relationships that are positive, healthy, fulfilling, and add value to my life.

I avoid spending time with people who are negative. I choose my friends wisely, and I surround myself with people who build me up and never put me down.

I do my best to keep from being critical. If someone has a problem, they already know it; if they want my advice, they'll ask for it.

I really like my life, and I like the people in it! I am good at building relationships, and I get better at it every day.

You deserve to have the best possible relationships, and with the right new Self-Talk programs in place, you can.

YOUR RELATIONSHIP WITH *YOU*

While we're on the subject of positive relationships, let's take the time to focus on a foundational relationship that sets up all the other relationships in your life. Other than a spiritual relationship, it is the relationship you have with *yourself* that is the most important, because all your other relationships begin with you.

Stop for a moment and consider who you would be if you had no one else in your life. In the next couple of pages, I'm going to gently and carefully lift away the layers of other people that you carry with you every day, in order to see what's there when you're all by yourself.

I promise not to dig too deep, or make you uncomfortable in any way. But there is an incredible power in the realization that who you are *underneath*, who you *really* are, is separate from whom you choose to be *with*.

WHO WOULD YOU BE,
IF YOU WERE STANDING ENTIRELY
ON YOUR OWN?

Our goal is to get to your true self, or at least to give you a glimpse of who she is and what she might look like if you gave her the chance to show herself more often. I'll take each area of relationships in turn, from where they all began.

Your parents

I'll start with your parents. Just for a moment, imagine your life without them. Whether your relationship with them is or was good or bad, positive or negative, pretend they no longer have any influence or direction in your life.

Do this whether they are living or not. It's critically

important to recognize that our parents' power over us doesn't automatically pass away when they do. I know many people who are still trying to live up to the expectations of a parent who died years ago! If you're doing that, and if it is working against you, it's time to get some new programs that will allow you to move on.

Go ahead, let yourself recognize that what your father thinks and what your mother thinks about who you are or what you should do, doesn't have to rule your life.

This in no way should take away from the respect and love you have for your parents, or from your gratitude for the positive gifts they have given you. I want to make this very clear.

But at the age of anywhere from about eighteen years to twenty-one years of age, depending on the society you grew up in, *you're* supposed to assume control of your own life—and that means your *parents* are supposed to let that control *go*.

If they, or you, have not yet accomplished this vital step in your growing-up process, no matter how old you are, you might want to take a closer look at your situation. It could be time for you to find a way to lovingly and carefully take the reins of your life into your own hands.

Your marriage

Next, let's pretend that even if you are currently married, you're not. I know that could feel uncomfortable, and I understand, so let me reassure you about one thing. We're going to put everything back in just a minute. It isn't my objective to get you to want a different life or a different marriage.

Rather, the *opposite* is true; when you have the courage to focus on who *you* are, and what *you* want, your husband is generally the winner, because he gains a more

116

contented wife. If you have one, mentally put your husband over to one side and, along with him, *everything he expects and assumes about the way you are.*

What are you doing that you think is for his sake or because he wants you to, that you'd rather not do? What challenges or dreams of yours have you buried or never mentioned because you think he won't let you pursue them?

I've known women who were deeply unhappy because they believed their husbands wanted them to be or act in a certain way, even when it wasn't true at all.

One of my friends, Lori, had a secret and strong yearning to go back to college as an adult. She was so certain that her husband wouldn't approve, or that her kids would resent her spending time away from home, that she never brought it up to them. Instead, she kept her dream bottled up inside her, never giving her family a chance to support her.

We had talked about it on several occasions, and I finally convinced her to tell her husband what she wanted to do. Not only was he pleasantly surprised that she had such a positive goal, he *and* the kids pitched in more around the house to make it possible for her to invest time in her schoolwork.

Lori got what she wanted, because she got *clear* about it, both with herself and with her family.

WHOSE FAULT IS IT
IF *YOU'RE* NOT HAPPY?

If, like Lori, you *do* start revealing the "real" you, you

may be surprised at the results. I'm not saying you will automatically get the same kind of support at home that enabled Lori to get her degree. But even if that doesn't happen, even if you have to stand up for your goals and dreams or make tradeoffs to get more of what you want, *it's better to be honest* with the people you love. Your life will probably work a lot better, and you'll be a lot happier being yourself than pretending your dreams don't matter.

If, like many women do, you've been silently thinking it's "all *his* fault," think again. If you've been blaming your husband for holding you back, *stop it*. You've got no one to blame but yourself if you aren't where you want to be in life. You married him; you ought to be able to trust him with the real you.

And while you're at it, give him the same courtesy you would hope for from him. Take the time to understand *his* dreams. Support him in *his* goals. Don't assume he's preventing you from becoming who you want to be—and make sure you stay out of the way of his progress, too. If you help each other, and work together on your goals, you'll both win.

Your friends and associates

All too often, we live our lives to impress or to please other people, even when we don't realize we're doing it.

What would your day look like, if you didn't have to do a single thing just because a friend or associate thought you should? What if they didn't exist?

How many activities are you undertaking, how much of your time do you give away when you'd rather have it for yourself or your family, how much work do you do to benefit someone other than yourself, and how long will you continue to let it be that way? What price do you

118

pay, just so other people will like you or to keep your current relationships the way they are?

It was quite a shock to me when I saw an example of a society that didn't live under the expectations we assume without question, thinking it's the only way.

I was in Arizona, on a tour of cave dwellings in an area of Indian ruins near Flagstaff. I'll never forget my amazement when the guide informed us that the cave dwellers spent an average of twenty hours a week for everything they needed to accomplish in order to sustain life: hunting, fishing, gathering and preparing food, maintaining safe shelter and raising their children.

Twenty hours a week. That's it. I know society has changed drastically since then, but I'm convinced there's a lesson to be learned here. I'm not suggesting you change everything in your life to a different lifestyle, but there *may* be alternatives.

What if there's another way? What if you're not forever tied to the way it *is*, just because that's the way it has always *been*?

Before we move on, picture your life without the obligations and expectations placed on you by your friends and associates. Do you *really* have to live with all those requirements from others, or can you find a way to lighten your load?

Everyone else

Now remove everyone else: your kids and their demands on you, your boss and what he or she expects from you in the course of a day, your sisters and brothers and how they make you feel and expect you to behave, even your mentors and role models, if you have any.

Now it's just you. In the final accounting, that's all you have anyway. You are born alone, and you will die that way too, and somewhere between the two, you must find your way for yourself.

In the rapid pace of our lives, most of us allow little time for self-examination, and some of us allow none at all. If nothing else, I encourage you to recognize that your life is precious. You deserve better, and if you disagree, go back and read the self-esteem section again.

Who are you, really—and what do you *really* want from your life? And what, if anything, are you going to do about it?

TAKE THE TIME
TO DUST OFF YOUR DREAMS

As busy as most of us are, we seldom have the time—or *allow ourselves* the time—to figure out what *we* want for ourselves. Instead, we live our lives day after day, from home to work to home and back again. In between are the children and the husband, the phone calls and the car pool, the dirty dishes and the dirty laundry and the *distractions* that take all our time and energy. It's no wonder *we* get lost in the shuffle!

Now and then there are moments, rare bits of time when we can pause and reflect. They happen to us at the most unexpected times—in line at the grocery store, when we hear a certain song that reminds us of an old boyfriend, when a new baby is born or a loved one dies, and sometimes for no reason at all.

Whether you call it "having the blues" or just "a bad day," whether you blame it on PMS or the weather or something you ate, whether it happens to you often or

120

not so frequently, the moment passes. The brief space of time—that second or two when you felt your old dream was almost within your grasp, when you believed for an instant that maybe you *could* make a change and make it work this time—goes away.

But what if you could hold onto that hope long enough to allow it to grow beyond a momentary wish that is quickly overridden by your "real" life? What if, just this once, it could be different?

Before you go on reading, before we take the next step of replacing the layers that make up your life, *stop*.

Put the book down. Go for a walk, go for a drive, go lie down—you choose—but go by yourself. Go think about who you are, where you are, what your life is like, and what, if anything, you would change if you could.

Take the time, have the courage, and give yourself the *permission* to think for a little while about your most heartfelt wishes, your most important hopes, your dearest dreams. If it has been too long since you have done this—or if you have never done it—and you can't remember what your dreams were, now is a great time to come up with some new ones.

Reclaim your life, if only for an hour or two. The rest of the world can wait, at least long enough for you to acknowledge that whatever your next move is, this time it's up to *you*.

LET'S PUT IT ALL BACK

Earlier, I promised that when we got through this section, I would put back the layers we lifted away so you could see the real you for a moment.

As we do, as you mentally re-assume the duties and obligations and roles and relationships of your life, think carefully about each one. Will you put them back in the same order? Will you do the same things? Will you choose to share the same amount of time with the same people?

Will you still say "yes" the next time the den mother calls you again and asks for four dozen cupcakes by four o'clock this evening?

Will you give in when your boss insists the ship will sink if you don't work late for the third time this week, or when your mother insists you have to come home for Christmas even though you're 47 years old and you'd rather go on a ski trip—or to Florida?

Or will you, the *real* you, finally have a say in the matter?

Don't misunderstand me. If you're happy with your life and every relationship in it, that's terrific. Don't change a thing. But if you're like most of us, it helps to stop now and then and examine your priorities, to make sure *you're* the one in control of your life.

Don't live your life by accident. Use the power of programming to make sure the relationships in your life are the right healthy ones that work *for* you, build you up, and help you in the pursuit of your dreams.

Choose to protect your home
and the well-being
of your family.

Never allow negativity
to live with you.

If you let a bad attitude
in the door,
it will bring its friends.

Make sure your home
is always
a positive place to be.

Chapter 10

SELF-TALK FOR BUILDING A STRONG FAMILY

*I*f you were to stand in the future, look back from the end of your life and focus on the life you had lived with your family, do you think you would wish you had done anything differently?

Is there anything you would change, if you had the chance to do it over again? Is there anything you would regret?

While you live, you have the opportunity to create the kind of family life you can later look back on with joy and pride.

Your relationship with your family, both with the family you were born into and the one you have now, is a valuable and precious thing. It's worth every effort you put in to make it stronger, more loving, and more like the family you want it to be.

No matter what your current family circumstances are,

you have the ability to improve them. No matter how difficult your "family problems" may seem, you can find a way to get past them. No matter how wide the gap is between your family and the ideal family, you have the opportunity to be the one to bridge that gap with your own new programs and behavior.

You have your own special place to fill. You are someone's daughter.

You are someone's sister, if you have siblings.

If you are married, you are someone's wife.

You are an aunt to your nieces and nephews; you are mother to your children or stepmother to your stepchildren. You may be a grandmother.

You may be all of these at once.

As a woman, as a wife, as a mother, as a daughter, as a sister, as an aunt or grandmother or stepmother, you play a special role in your family. Even if you are biologically alone in the world, you can build a loving family with the people who are closest to you. They *need* you. More important, they need *you*.

You are a vital link in the chain that holds the structure of your family together, even if you haven't seen yourself that way in the past.

YOU CAN MAKE A FAMILY WHEREVER YOU ARE

If you have not been blessed with a close family circle of people who are related to you by blood, that doesn't mean you have to do without a family. Some of the most loving environments of all are those created by people who structure a family by choice.

One of the most difficult times of my life turned out to be one of the most fulfilling, because of the "family" that developed by accident.

I had left the active duty military to go back to school in order to earn my credentials as an officer. My life changed overnight. It felt like going backward—and even though I knew that at times we all have to backtrack in order to move forward, it was hard to accept. All I could do was hold onto my faith that I was doing the right thing, and step out to meet my future.

I called my father's sister, my Aunt Jean, whom I had seen only occasionally during the previous few years. We didn't know each other well; all she knew was that I needed a place to stay while I was in school. It was a great relief to me when Aunt Jean said, "Yes. You can come and live with me."

Over the next months, Aunt Jean and I became very close. She and I and her wonderful black Labrador, Velvet, became a family. Money was tight, but we would spend what we had to cook special treats for each other, to cheer ourselves up after a long or particularly tiring day. Velvet would wait for us to get home, her head resting on her paws as she gazed out the living room window. The dog had learned to stand on her hind paws and "hug" us when we walked in the door.

I met my husband Shad while I was still in school, and I knew without a doubt what all the hardship and waiting had been for. When it came time for him to propose to me, Shad made the right move: he asked Aunt Jean if it would be okay with her. Fortunately for us both, she agreed.

126

I have a larger family now, one that includes not only my parents and sisters and their children, but also my husband and his parents and his brothers and sisters and *their* children.

Aunt Jean is still a big part of my life, even though I don't get to see her as often as I would like. Velvet is no longer with us, but I remember her love and her hugs as a rare blessing.

I still miss that dog.

IT BEGINS WITH YOU

In every family, it seems at least one individual is the "glue" that holds everything in place. I'm talking about that person who seems to make everything go more smoothly, just because he or she is in the room. This is the person who holds the love and shares it most freely with the other members of the family—the person without whom the family circle would be most incomplete.

I'm talking about the one who has the family's heart. In many cases, that role is naturally assumed by a woman, because it is traditionally and biologically our job to comfort, love, and encourage the people we care about. We're biologically, chemically designed to be that way. We have a special position, and we tend to do our best and be our happiest when we are able to fulfill this side of our lives.

If you are a woman who feels the role of wife and mother is not for you, I'm not here to argue with you.

But I *am* going to encourage you to allow time for your nurturing side, because if you don't, you're missing out on some of the best moments life has to offer.

Even if you don't think you're that special family person now, you can *become* the kind of person that everyone in your family will naturally turn to. You can choose to set the tone for your family, by your attitude, your actions, and the standards you set for yourself.

WHAT IF YOU'VE ALREADY GOT IT RIGHT?

If you *are* already the kind of warm, loving woman I've been describing, I commend you. You give hope to the rest of us, and make everyone feel better just by being around you. Keep doing it.

If you are already happy with the way your family life is going, it will still help to have plenty of good Self-Talk ammunition ready when the challenges come up. The world today is a far different environment for our children than it was for us when we were growing up. It's not being negative to acknowledge that it is harder to raise good kids these days; it's the truth.

You owe it to yourself and to your family to build the strongest family unit you can. It's what you have when you close the door on the world at night, when you are alone with yourself and the ones you've chosen to share your life with, that matters the most.

SELF-TALK FOR YOUR FAMILY

The following programs of Self-Talk are designed to help you create and maintain a strong, healthy, loving family environment. If you already have one, these new programs will help you build on the foundation you've set in place. And if you're not yet where you'd like to be where your family is concerned, this is the Self-Talk that can help you get there.

Self-Talk for Building a Strong Family

I make my family a priority in my life. I protect it, I work at it, and I build it.

I am proud of my family, and I make sure I live my life each day in a way that makes them proud of me.

When I choose to make sacrifices for the people I love, I do it gladly. I am willing to give of myself to make my family's life a better place to be.

I am building a life that works. I have hope for the future, joy in the present, and faith in my family.

I never wait for another day, or a later time, to tell my family how much I love them. My time with them is precious and important, and I let them know it.

In my family, I choose to set the example for others to follow. I do what I need to do to keep myself strong, so my family can always count on me.

129

I have learned to celebrate the differences between me and the other members of my family. Even in times of temporary stress or difficulty, I always show them an attitude of love and respect.

I have something special to offer to every person in my family, and I make it a point to spend time with each of them.

I protect my home and the well-being of my family. I never allow negativity to live with me, because I know if I let a bad attitude in the door, it will bring its friends. So I make sure my home is always a positive place to be.

I choose to be the glue that holds my family together. I will never give up on them, and I know they will always be there for me, too.

When my family faces challenges, I stay calm, focused, and in control.

I am a leader. I always show my family a person they can honor and respect, and I do all I can to help them set the highest possible standards for their own lives.

I work hard to build and maintain a strong family circle, and it is worth every bit of the effort and dedication I give it. To me, my family is a precious blessing, and I am thankful for it every day.

I never let outside interests or friendships get in the way of building a life for my family. I save the best of me for the ones I love most.

Every day, I get better at being the kind of person that makes my family shine. Because my family is special, other people notice—and they want to be where we are.

My family knows my dreams, and I know theirs. I keep my heart and my eyes open for ways to make their lives even better. And when I see a way to add happiness, I do what it takes to make it happen for them.

My life is good, because of my family; my family is strong, because I work to make it that way.

That's the kind of Self-Talk that can make every day of your family's life work better!

WHAT CAN YOU DO, BEGINNING TODAY?

You have the opportunity in front of you to begin building the kind of family atmosphere you'd most like to have. It starts with you, with your attitude and the way you choose to present yourself. Program *yourself* first, to be the kind of person your family can most admire—then begin to share it with each of them.

There are as many ways to start giving your family members positive programs as there are moments in your day. Think of it in terms of typing important messages into their computer keyboards, and use your imagination.

Don't be hesitant to write the note that tells your husband you believe in him, or make the call to invite your brother to lunch, even though you've never really gotten along that well. Go ahead and send the flowers or the simple card that says, "I believe in you."

Everything you do, everything you say to the people you care about most, is being *programmed* into their computers and will help them form a picture of who they are. Once you know how, you can start immediately typing in the best possible programs. Even if they don't know exactly *what* it is that's different about you, your family will respond and grow because of you.

A WORD ABOUT YOUR KIDS

What I'm going to say next applies to you, even if you don't have children of your own.

I implore you to be particularly careful with the programs you give to the children in your life! I don't mean that you should be afraid to open your mouth for fear of saying the wrong thing and doing irreparable damage. Rather, look at the positive side of the same situation.

What can you offer to the kids you care about? What messages of belief and hope and love and potential can you give *them*?

This is especially true with your own children, because you are the guardian of their moral, spiritual, and emotional well-being. It's your sacred duty to equip those young hearts and minds for a life well-lived, *even if you didn't get taught properly yourself.*

You may not have been given all the building blocks of

values and character that your children need. And because of the way programming works, you may not know which ones you lack. I'm sure you have the best intentions in the world, and want the best for your kids, and you will give them the best of what you got.

If you were fortunate enough to be raised in a strong family environment, you have much of what is needed to pass on to your kids. We pass along the programs we got, without having to think about the process. But what if you weren't raised in the best environment? Or what if you are missing some of the programs your kids need to progress and grow? Here's how to bridge that gap.

WHERE ARE YOUR CHILDREN GETTING THEIR PROGRAMS NOW?

Even if your own programs growing up weren't the best, you can give better programs to your kids than your parents gave you. The answer to this problem has two parts:

1. Give *yourself* the right new programs of values, character, and integrity, so you pass along the *right* programs to your children.

2. Make sure your children have the right *outside* influences in their lives, so their *other* programs are also the best they can get.

By reading this book and working on building new Self-

Talk programs, you're addressing the first part of that process.

The second part is equally important. It's up to you to manage, as much as you possibly can, the *sources of input from which your children get their programs.*

If you want your kids to have strong, positive programs that will serve them well for the rest of their lives, here's my list of recommendations:

o **Limit the amount of television programming your kids are allowed to watch.** Better yet, eliminate it almost entirely. (This could sound extreme unless you remember that *all* input they are getting is programmed in for life and acted on as if it were true.) When in doubt, *turn it off.*

o **Encourage your kids to read, even if you're not a reader yourself.** Some of the best program role models are found in the simple stories of good children's books, and the great works of literature. Start small, and work your way up—and read *with* them, if you can.

o **Spend time with other adults that share your values.** Some of the strongest programs your kids get come from watching what you do and who you spend your time with. Make sure you show them a good example. You'll do better, and so will they, if your friends reflect the best of you.

o **Find a church home, and go there with your kids.** It's not my place to tell you what to believe, but I've witnessed a dramatic difference in the lives of kids who have a strong spiritual foundation, and those who don't. Some of the strongest families of all are the families who share a belief system that guides their behavior, both day-to-day and long-term. If you've never tried this one, I recommend you give it another look.

o **Make sure your children's teachers understand the concept of programming.** Your kids get much more than reading, writing, and arithmetic at school. They get important programs that, unless you choose to home school your children, they don't get from you. Take the time to talk to each of the teachers who are giving your kids their programs. If you don't agree with their approach, find another school.

o **Don't be afraid to choose what kind of friends your children have.** This is a tough one for many parents, because kids today are more independent and more determined than ever to run their own lives at an early age. Granted, it takes energy and effort to monitor what kind of friends your kids choose, but it can be done—and the grief they give you now if you guide their choices for them is much easier to deal with than the heartache that can come later if you don't.

o **Make sure the other members of your extended family and your childcare givers are aware of the way you're raising your kids.** The most well-meaning relatives can often do the most damage to your children. If you have set down certain rules for your kids, and other adult members of your family allow them to break these rules, it's time to set it straight. The same applies to *anyone* who has access to your children's keyboards on a regular basis. Your kids are *your* responsibility, and if they're getting the wrong programs from other adults in their lives, it's your job to stop that from happening.

As you see, you can and should have a say in *every* aspect of the programs your family receives.

It could seem demanding to be the self-appointed caretaker of your family's programs. Yes, it takes energy, but the results are more than worthwhile.

It actually gets *easier*, once the new base programs are in place. Remember, your strongest programs create more like them, and once you start building the programs you want, the process takes off on its own.

Every day,
take small steps toward
your fitness goals.

Before you know it,
you'll get where you're
going.

Chapter 11

SELF-TALK FOR
HEALTH AND FITNESS

*T*his subject is the single area that contains more negative programs for women than any other. Just mention the word "fitness" to an average group of women and watch their response.

For most of us, it's much too easy to believe that in this area, we simply don't measure up. We are somehow convinced that everyone *else* around us is way ahead when it comes to health, and fitness in particular.

We know exercise is "good for us." We know we're supposed to "eat right." We've been programmed and programmed and programmed with pictures in magazines and words and looks at the dinner table and size tags on dresses that tell us how we "ought" to look.

I don't know about you, but *I'm* sick and tired of other people trying to set my fitness standards for me!

It took me years and years of my life to get past this one

138

and get to the point where I felt secure enough to decide for *myself* how I wanted to look and feel.

It helped me a great deal to recognize that when it comes to determining my health and fitness level, *I'm* in charge—and no one else has the right or the responsibility to take that control away from me.

WHO IS SETTING YOUR STANDARD?

For a long time, I allowed myself to buy into the false image of the "perfect woman" that we see every day on billboards and magazine covers. *You* may be a flawless size six with slender but shapely hips, pouty lips, hair that falls into place with a toss of your head, dazzlingly white and perfectly straight teeth, legs up to your neck, a tiny waist, a gravity-free behind, and breasts to die for—but most of us don't fall into that category!

So why *is* it that we suffer and grieve and beat ourselves up for our imagined faults and failings when it comes to being fit and healthy? Why are we so hard on ourselves—and what can we do about it?

What I finally did, that worked for me, was to decide once and for all that I would set my standards for *myself*. I worked on Self-Talk for self-esteem along with specific new programs of health and fitness that painted a *realistic* picture of me as a healthy person. The Self-Talk helped me stop buying into everyone *else's* image of how I should look, how much I should weigh, and what kind and frequency of exercise was right for me.

I'm not going to pretend it was easy to get rid of the

shackles of a lifetime of advertising images that told me I could never look good enough. It wasn't easy. But with the right focus on new programs, it got better.

GIVE YOURSELF NEW PROGRAMS ABOUT YOUR HEALTH AND FITNESS

The following script of Self-Talk is designed to help you learn to see yourself as a fit and healthy person. If you focus on building these kinds of programs, and add a healthy dose of new self-esteem programs as well, you should begin to see yourself improving in this area.

You will more than likely *look* better by focusing on your healthy self, and you will certainly *feel* better. Here's the Self-Talk.

Self-Talk for Health and Fitness

I am a healthy person, and I know that's the best way for me to be.

Every day, I take small steps toward my fitness goals—and before I know it, I get where I'm going!

I never quit. I never give up. I never stop. And I succeed.

I take charge of my health, and I make sure I do everything I can to be as healthy as I possibly can.

Whenever I think the word "exercise," I automatically and naturally picture the joy of creating my very best self.

I spend time with others who share my fitness goals, and encourage me to stay with it.

I never make excuses. I get up, I get out, and I get it done!

I enjoy eating the foods that are the best for my body. I take care of my body, and it takes care of me.

Other people see me as a positive example of fitness and health—and I show them my best effort, all the time.

If there is ever a moment when it seems difficult to be healthy, I go past the moment and keep my attitude up in spite of it.

I know that an important part of my fitness is the shape of my spirit, so I do everything I can to protect and nurture both my body and my soul.

Tomorrow is another day. I do what I can do today, but I also remember that tomorrow is another opportunity for me to create positive fitness and health in my life.

I find joy in small accomplishments, because I know that all those healthy moments add up.

I always have plenty of energy; in fact, I always have more than I need.

Instead of focusing too much on the size or shape my body is in, I stay in tune with the size and shape of my attitude, my personality, my goals, and my success.

If I am ever discouraged, I work on keeping a positive perspective. When I keep my eye on the future, today always looks brighter!

I may not see the results of today's effort, today—but next month and next year will be healthier for me because I'm investing in myself right now.

Each day, I can see more of that healthy, happy person I was born to be. I'm making progress, and it shows!

You *are* making progress, just by being aware of the programs that control your fitness and health.

WHAT IF YOU
WANT TO LOSE WEIGHT?

That script of Self-Talk for health and fitness is the one to use, in particular, if losing weight is an issue for you. You may have noticed that I haven't said much about weight in this chapter, even though it is the section on fitness and health.

There's a reason for that. The fact is, most of the problems women have with weight are actually the result of problems we're having with something *else*—self-esteem, difficulty in a relationship, problems at work or at home, and so on. Eating too much is almost *always* the result of trying to address the needs of other areas of our lives. Even though it works against us, when we have that empty feeling—*no matter what caused it in the first place*—we try to fill the void with food.

The *issues* that put the extra weight on, and keep it on, *especially* for women, are seldom issues of health, and usually have nothing to do with food, except indirectly. If you want to lose weight, it's good to work with this script of programs about your overall health, but you should *also* focus on the areas of self-esteem, relationships, goals, and energy and enthusiasm, to name a few.

If losing weight has been difficult for you in the past, there's hope—if you keep taking the appropriate healthy steps of the right diet and exercise plan, and give yourself the right new mental programs. With the addition of strong positive Self-Talk about who you are and what you can do, you can build the programs that allow you to finally see yourself as a naturally slender and healthy person who deserves to stay that way.

I've seen Self-Talk do wonders in this area, for me and for many others, and if you want to take control of your weight once and for all, I encourage you to make your new programs an integral part of your fitness plan. If you lose your old programs, the weight often goes with them.

MY "TOP 10" FOR LIVING A HEALTHY LIFE

I've encountered many good hints and ideas in the pursuit of my lifelong goal to be healthy. I've narrowed them down to ten of my most favorite steps I've used in order to be happier, feel better, and live a healthier life. I hope they help you as much as they have helped me.

1. Get rid of the guilt. The Self-Talk phrase that helped me most with this is, "*I no longer live my life based on the negative opinions of others.*" Try it—it works.

2. Remember that little steps add up. Don't try to do it all at once. Do a little every day, or even every other day or once a week. A year from now, you'll be much healthier than if you had done nothing.

3. Focus on how you feel, instead of how you look. Don't worry about what size the tag says; buy and wear the clothes that fit and feel comfortable. People will respond better to you if they can see you are at ease with yourself, and that begins with setting yourself free from the belief that you have to live up to someone else's ideal of how you look. Choose for yourself, and *relax*!

4. Remember to smile. When you do, it makes *any* body look better, no matter what shape that body is in. Besides, you create positive, *healthy* chemical changes in your brain every time you smile.

5. Take vitamins. I do. Every day, more than once a day, and I can feel my energy drop when I don't. I'm not a doctor, but I can figure out that Linus Pauling, who shared the secret of Vitamin C with the rest of us, lived into his nineties for a *reason*. In particular, I think it's a good idea to take at least a multivitamin and extra Vitamin C, especially if you smoke. (And as for smoking, you've heard enough about that; *that* one is so obvious it doesn't even need to be on my list.)

6. Spend time with people who encourage you to be healthy. Too many of our so-called friends are the kind of people who sabotage our fitness efforts. Try to save your free time to be with people who help you instead of harm you. It may seem hard to change your friends, but if you avoid the nay-sayers, you'll feel and do a lot better.

7. Never say you're going to catch a cold, or any other kind of illness. With every word you say, you're giving *instructions* to your body! It's okay to listen to your body and get the rest and medicine you need, but make sure *you're* in charge of your body, and not the other way around. It's better for your *body* to listen to *you*.

8. Go for a walk. If I could get you to change only one thing about your fitness routine, it would be to get you to walk. It's natural, easy, and free, and you can do it anytime, anywhere. Start with a short walk and progress at your own pace. Again, focus on how you *feel*, and don't buy into the expectations of anyone (including *yourself*) that you ought to walk faster, or run. Just enjoy yourself.

9. Eat what you want. This could sound counter-productive, but I've learned that it works. Our society's obsession with "fat-free" has robbed us of the taste of good food, so we eat much more than we ought to in a

145

vain attempt to satisfy our hunger. If you want to reach your natural, healthy weight and stay there, I found that it works better to eat real food, in normal healthy amounts. It's *amazing*—your body will actually tell you when it's full, and with the right healthy new programs in place to help you, *you can stop eating too much.*

10. Be proud of what you do. Once and for all, stop worrying about what you *didn't* do. We women are much too hard on ourselves. Instead of focusing on where you fell short (and whose expectations are you trying to live up to, anyway?), be proud of what you accomplished. Build a new habit of self-confidence and contentment, and your fitness will naturally follow.

A LITTLE IMPROVEMENT
CAN TAKE YOU A LONG WAY

I don't expect you to make any radical changes in your diet or exercise plan, just from reading this book and getting some new, healthy mental programs. My objective is to encourage you to see your fitness and health in a new way, so you can build on your successes.

Self-Talk isn't designed to get you to do anything drastic. The simpler a solution is, the better it will work. The goal of learning new Self-Talk for health and fitness is to help you break the negative cycle of despair and failure created by diets that don't work, exercise plans that last a few days (or a few hours!), and the unrealistic expectations created by everyone from the media to your friends and family members.

With the right Self-Talk programs, you'll be able to start and maintain a gradual, step-by-step journey on the road to lifelong fitness and health. The idea is to make *small* changes that *add up*. Even a minor improvement in an area of your life that has been worrying you will make a major difference in the quality of your life day by day.

*If you can't change
the <u>circumstances</u>
of a stressful situation,
you can always
change your <u>attitude</u>.*

*The situation
will be the same.*

*It is your <u>programs</u>
that will make the difference.*

Chapter 12

SELF-TALK FOR REDUCING STRESS

*W*e all have responsibilities. Every one of us has to answer to *someone*. That will probably never change. Those obligations will always be there.

Even if you can't change the situation, what you *can* change is your attitude about the way you deal with the stress creators in your life. We've all seen people who handle stress better than others, even when faced with the same problems. And the difference is more than just personality; the difference is in the *programs* of how they deal with the stress in the first place.

WHAT DOES SHE KNOW
THAT YOU DON'T?

You probably know at least one woman in your life who seems to sail through even the most difficult circumstances and still stay calm. This is the woman who seems to have a life just like yours, but she somehow deals with it better, and seems to be happier than you feel.

What is her secret, this calm and happy woman? How does she handle situations that well when you can't? What does *she* know that you *don't*? And how can you attain more of the peace of mind that she seems to have in abundance?

To illustrate the difference I'm talking about, I'll use the example of Lynn and Kelly. These two women are of a similar age and income, and their jobs are similar, too. Each of them is married, both work outside the home, and both have small children. Most important, their *personalities* are similar. Both are intelligent, articulate, energetic women who want to do well in their lives.

To listen to Kelly talk, her life is one stressful moment after another. A readout of her programs would closely resemble some of the statements from the "Hot 100" list we looked at earlier. Lynn, on the other hand, has many more of the right programs on her side, and it makes a real difference in her stress level.

Let's examine a typical day in the lives of these two women. Let's see where their stress comes from, and how each of them chooses to deal with it.

THE DAY IS THE SAME; IT'S THE *PROGRAMS* THAT ARE DIFFERENT

The alarm goes off at five-thirty on Wednesday morning. Kelly reaches out and hits the snooze button, mumbling *"Just ten more minutes!"* under her breath as she rolls over and goes back to sleep.

Lynn is just as sleepy, but she automatically swings her feet over the side of the bed and puts them on the floor, heading for the shower before she is fully awake. *"I can do this,"* she says quietly to herself, even though she didn't want to get out of bed any more than Kelly did.

At six o'clock, Kelly has just made it to the shower, and is having to rush because her four-year-old son is pounding on the bathroom door demanding his breakfast. *"It's going to be another one of those days,"* she mutters.

At that same time, Lynn is in the kitchen fixing breakfast for her small daughter. Her hair and makeup are done because she gave herself the extra half-hour of private time she needed so she wouldn't have to hurry. *"I really feel great today,"* she says out loud to herself, packing the lunch bags as her daughter finishes eating.

AS THE MORNING GOES, SO GOES THE DAY

By the time Kelly gets to work, she has a run in her stocking that she snagged while hurrying to put gas in the car. She's running late and looks it. *"I can never catch up,"* she moans as she dashes in the door, passing her boss on her way to the elevator. He looks at his watch, noticing she's late for the second time that week. *"Just my luck,"* Kelly says.

Lynn put gas in her car the night before, so she has plenty of time to swing through the drive-through and pick up some cinnamon rolls to bring to the office. *"I really like doing special things for people,"* she thinks to herself, humming along with the song on the radio. She's smiling when she arrives early at work, and her boss notices her punctuality, as usual. *"What a great day!"* she says.

THE CYCLE CONTINUES

By the end of the day, Kelly hates her life and everyone in it. She's tired, cranky, and wishes she could be anywhere else, and any*one* else, while she's at it. *"Sometimes I just want to quit,"* she complains on the way home from work. *"Nothing ever goes right for me!"*

Lynn, on the other hand, has plenty of energy left when she gets home. She had to work just as hard, but somehow things went better for her that day than they did for Kelly. *"I'm really lucky,"* she thinks as she looks back on her day, and sees the direction her life is going. *"Things always seem to work out right for me."*

Kelly and Lynn, at first glance, had the same kind of life—but there was one vital difference. Each woman created a cycle of behavior and attitude with the way they approached their day, but one way worked, and the other didn't. One was a positive cycle, and the other was negative.

It's important to note that Lynn's successful day wasn't just luck, and she didn't start out being automatically positive and on top of the world. She had to learn what worked and change accordingly.

To listen to her tell it, Lynn's life used to be at least as difficult and unrewarding as Kelly's. "I was stressed all the time," she says. "Something had to give, because I didn't have anything *left* to give. I was all used up—I felt like an old woman, and I wasn't even thirty yet!"

Lynn was able to break the cycle of stress, because she figured out that she needed to change her programs about the way she was living her life. Along with new programs of self-esteem and setting goals, Lynn worked on building new mental program pathways for dealing with stress, programs that would allow her to become the calm and happy person she was born to be.

WHICH KIND OF DAY SOUNDS MORE LIKE YOURS?

As you read this section of Self-Talk, think about what your own programs in this area currently are. Are you fortunate enough to be more like Lynn, or does Kelly's story ring a bell?

Wherever you are on the contentment scale, the following Self-Talk script can help you find ways to conquer the stress that's been holding you down.

Self-Talk for Reducing Stress

I practice remaining calm, no matter what the situation.

I never let someone else's negativity pull me down. I control my own attitude, and no one else ever controls it for me.

I allow time for myself, so I never mind the time it takes to get things done.

I have learned to delegate, and I allow others to help me make my life better by keeping my day free of stress.

If I find myself feeling negative pressure, I walk away for a moment. I clear my mind, and then I begin again.

I know that maintaining my own mental clarity is the best thing I can do to improve any circumstance.

I never take myself or my life too seriously. I have fun!

Even when it's difficult, I keep my sense of humor—and my positive outlook makes everything work better for me.

I spend my time with optimistic people, and I achieve peace of mind by following their example.

I focus my energy and emotion on the things that matter, instead of wasting them on the things that don't.

If I need help, I ask for it sooner, not later.

I observe other people, and I practice styles that work for them. I'm always "me," but I learn from others, and I grow when I do.

154

Each time I come through a difficult situation with my attitude intact, I congratulate myself for having done it right.

Every day that goes by, I am stronger, calmer, and more in control of myself and my life.

I keep a long-term perspective. Because I am always looking ahead and reaching for my next goal, the problems of today never get me down.

I enjoy feeling calm and happy. I choose to be contented in all that I do.

Does that sound like you? It can, if you work at giving yourself that kind of positive program reinforcement!

The next time you face a stressful situation, choose a favorite line of that kind of Self-Talk to keep handy. For now, even before you've learned how to make *all* the Self-Talk a permanent part of your life, say the Self-Talk out loud, right in the middle of the problem, and watch what happens next.

It might not make the challenge go away, but at least you'll know you're doing everything you can to protect your attitude and your day. You'll set the right cycle in motion, instead of the wrong one.

At the moment, it's enough that you're reading and becoming familiar with the right kind of Self-Talk about dealing with stress.

As with each of the areas of Self-Talk, by the time you get to the section of actual techniques for you to practice to build your new programs, you'll have a good feel for the way your new programs on this subject should sound.

In the next chapter, we're going to look at more ways to get programs that will make you feel great, help you get more done in a day, and help you to have an overall positive approach to your life. It's time to give you new programs of *energy and enthusiasm*.

*Don't hold back
from enjoying today,
<u>today.</u>*

*Each day
will bring with it
the renewed energy you need
to make the most
of every moment
you are given.*

Chapter 13

SELF-TALK FOR ENERGY AND ENTHUSIASM

*D*o you always have the kind of energy you'd like to have, or do you run out of steam before you run out of hours in the day? Would you like to be more alive and enthusiastic, more cheerful and optimistic and going for it?

If you want to do that, you can.

Even if you aren't used to having an abundance of energy, there are some things you can do to get more done with the energy you *do* have.

WHERE ENERGY AND ENTHUSIASM COME FROM

Your "energy" determines how much you can get done in any given day, and it comes from a combination of things. Your energy level is partly genetic; it was predetermined along with your hair, your eye color and your body type.

After that, you affect your energy with the amount of rest you get, the kind and quantity of the food you eat, what your activities are, the quality of your environment, the people you spend your time with, and of course, the programs you give yourself about what you believe you can do—in short, your *attitude*.

Your level of enthusiasm could, at first, seem to be pretty much the same thing—how energetically you tackle anything you do. But that's only partly true.

The word "enthusiasm" comes from the Greek *entheos*, which means "God within."

Your enthusiasm is a direct representation of what kind of *spirit* you have inside you—the spirit that tells you and everyone else around you how you feel about life, and how happy you are (or aren't) to be living that life.

Enthusiasm, too, comes from a variety of sources. It comes from God, from the positive feeling you get when you accomplish what you set out to do, from the people you surround yourself with, from the goals you set and your pursuit of those goals, and from your programs about what kind of life you think you can have.

WHAT KIND OF PERSON WOULD YOU RATHER BE?

We've all known people who make us feel tired and down, just by their own lack of energy. In contrast are those rare individuals who make everyone around them feel revitalized and glad to be alive.

Most of us are somewhere in between, and unless you're the kind of person who already has energy and enthusiasm to spare, you can benefit from the following Self-Talk. If you *are* already that positive person, read it and enjoy the picture of yourself that you're presenting to the rest of us!

Here's a new set of Self-Talk programs that can help you boost your level of energy and enthusiasm. Read this script now, and keep it close at hand to read again anytime you're about to face a particularly trying or tiring situation. This is the kind of Self-Talk that, if you decide to use the techniques for reprogramming we'll learn later, will become a natural and automatic part of who you are.

Self-Talk for Energy and Enthusiasm

I love being alive! I always find the good in my day, and I build from there. I turn ordinary days into incredible days!

I never worry what someone else thinks of my attitude—because my attitude is always great.

I approach any task with the expectation of a positive outcome, so that's what I get.

When I am tired, I rest. I don't complain.

I work hard, I play hard, and I appreciate every moment of joy that comes my way.

People like me. I smile a lot, and they respond to me by treating me better than ever.

I have energy! I am enthusiastic, full of vitality, and glad to be alive!

I lead by example. My optimism brings out the best in the people around me, and my own day goes better because of the positive cycle I create.

I always give myself the Self-Talk that builds my attitude and my energy!

I avoid those activities that steal my time and energy while offering nothing worthwhile in return. I focus instead on the people, the places, and the pastimes that feed my spirit and help me grow.

I build my energy with exercise and healthy fitness, and I feel better every day.

I make time for quiet activities that renew my spirit and bring me peace of mind.

I spend my time with others who share my enthusiastic approach to life, and the friendships I build are second to none.

My warmth draws others to me, and my loving spirit keeps them there.

I know that part of managing my energy is knowing when to quit.

My life is in balance. I give my best effort to everything I do, and when it is time to rest, I rest assured, knowing I have done all I can do.

I don't hold back from enjoying today, today. I know that each new day will bring with it the renewed energy I will need to make the most of every moment I am given.

My goals create energy and enthusiasm in my life. I have an upbeat outlook on life, because I am always looking out for my next accomplishment. I'm on my way!

When you build strong programs about energy and enthusiasm, your day will naturally go better, and you'll accomplish more of what you set out to do.

Let's take a closer look at some of the ways you can preserve the energy and enthusiasm you already have, and the ways you can get more of both.

THE COMPANY YOU KEEP

Nothing can steal your energy faster than being around someone who is constantly negative or complaining. Even though we know the fault lies with the programs instead of with the person, we suffer anytime we're forced to spend time with someone like that.

If you want to have more energy, if you want to approach each day with a positive and enthusiastic attitude, you must protect yourself from those who take your energy from you and give you nothing in return.

If those "energy stealers" are your friends, you have a choice. I recommend you begin to limit the amount of time you spend with them. The best choice of all would be to seek out and spend time with friends who add to your energy instead.

Sometimes, though, you don't have a choice about the people in your immediate vicinity. If you work with someone who brings you down on a regular basis, or worse yet, if you must *live* with someone like that, it's more difficult to avoid the problem.

WHAT CAN YOU DO
TO HELP SOMEONE WHO IS NEGATIVE?

The biggest mistake most of us make in this situation is that we wear ourselves out trying vainly to prop up the energy and attitude of the person who is down.

If you've been trying that approach, I have to tell you from painful experience that it cannot work. You'll only burn yourself out in the process.

What I suggest you try instead is to first make sure your own programs are strong, especially in the areas of how you deal with stress, your self-esteem, and your relationships. After that, you can share your new-found Self-Talk with the other people in your life who might need some help rebuilding their own mental highways so they can travel in a better direction.

If you do that, they will win, and so will you. *They'll* win because if they have better programs, they'll see life differently, and they will eventually stop behaving in a way that constantly works against them. And *you'll* win because you're no longer wasting your energy trying to prop up someone else who is negative. You will have removed the source of your energy drain, and you can use that restored energy to get on with your life.

LEARN TO SAY "NO"

Along with spending time with negative or complaining people, another way we women give away our precious energy and destroy our enthusiasm is by taking on too heavy a load of obligations. If this sounds like you, then in order to regain your energy and enthusiasm, you have to learn to pick and choose which things you'll agree to do, and which ones you'll refuse.

This can be very difficult for women. We are taught from an early age to be the ones to please others, to be "nice," to smooth things over, to *yield*.

I'm not encouraging you to become selfish in a negative way, or to break the essential habit of having and using good manners. But this particular problem, the inability to say "no" when you need to, is a primary reason why you take care of everyone *else's* needs first, and your own needs last—if your needs get taken care of at all.

In order to break this particular habit, it helps to figure out who is in charge of setting your priorities for you.

Who is in control of your time? Who gets to determine what you do, and what you don't do?

All too often, as women, our old programs regulate how we use our time and energy. We follow the old, negative, guilty voices in our heads that say if we don't agree to do such-and-such, then so-and-so won't like us, or we won't measure up, or the sky will fall.

But will it really?

Will your life truly suffer if you turn down that friend who's been trying to get you to join the health club with her, or if you don't wash that sink full of dishes until later, or if you stay at home and take a much-needed nap instead of taking the neighborhood kids to soccer practice?

You can come up with plenty of examples of your own, I'm sure. But it's *fascinating* what happens to your energy level when you change your programs enough that you allow yourself to start taking things *off* your list!

IT HELPS TO FIGURE OUT
WHAT IS REALLY IMPORTANT TO YOU

I began to reassess my priorities when I finally reached a point where I realized I wouldn't have enough time in this life to accomplish everything I'd wanted to. If that hasn't yet happened to you, I can tell you that it's very interesting when it does.

My 35th birthday was my own personal wake-up call. I was in New York, sitting in my hotel room and looking down onto the bright lights of Times Square. I was thinking about how much I enjoyed the city, and I was looking forward to spending the evening of my birthday with my husband and a couple of close friends.

We had come to the city to be with our friends and to see a Broadway show or two. I love theater, and the shows on Broadway are pure magic to me. I don't go as often as I would like, so it means a lot when I do.

It occurred to me as I sat there that *half my life was over*. I wondered how many more plays I would see, how many more trips to New York remained in my lifetime, how much more time I would be able to spend with my friends.

It could have depressed me to think in those terms, but instead, it made me appreciate how valuable the good times in my life are to me. It made me more determined than ever to create and protect time in my life to spend with people I care about, doing the things I love to do.

All of a sudden, it gets easier to set your priorities for yourself, when you figure out you only have so much time left.

MAKE SURE YOU PUT YOUR ENERGY IN THE RIGHT PLACE

A young woman named Marcia shared with me what happened when her husband decided to go into business for himself.

"At first, I was opposed to the idea," she said. "Steve had gotten his degree with a perfect 4.0 grade point average in his major of business pre-law, which meant he could pretty much choose the law school he wanted to attend. When he told me he wanted to start his own business instead of going on to law school, I thought he was making a big mistake. I wanted a secure future, and I thought the best way to do that was the way we had planned, with both of us getting good jobs after college.

"It dawned on me that Steve might have a better idea when someone showed me what having a job would really mean over the course of a lifetime. I was 23 years old at the time, which meant I had at least 40 years to go in order to reach retirement. That meant it would use up more than *fourteen thousand* days of my life to get to the point where I could retire!

"And even then, I would have nothing to show for it but a pension check. I figured out right then and there that it was better to spend my energy helping my husband build the business, so we would do better financially and create something our kids would be able to inherit, too."

The last time we talked, Marcia was no longer working for an outside boss and was working full-time to help her husband move forward. She and Steve have built a very successful business, and they're well on their way to creating a financially secure future that doesn't depend on outside employment. Best of all, at their current rate of progress, they can *both* plan on retirement long before they reach their 60's.

Marcia demonstrates more energy and enthusiasm than any three other women I know. Part of her secret is that she figured out a way to use her energy that would give her something worthwhile in return, instead of following a path that failed to reward her efforts. She bought her energy back, and every day of her life is better because she did.

HOW MUCH TIME AND *ENERGY* DO YOU HAVE LEFT?

Take a moment and figure out your own equation. Let's assume the average age for a woman's life expectancy is somewhere in the late 70's. Now let's give you the benefit of the doubt, and assume you're going to live a long, healthy life (especially since you'll have all the right mental programs working in your favor).

Let's say you will live to be 83 years of age. If you are now 37, that means you have 46 years to go, or just less than seventeen thousand days of time left to do whatever it is you want to accomplish in your lifetime.

If you are 47, you've got about thirteen thousand days to go, and if you're 50 or older, that leaves you with twelve thousand or fewer.

My point in this exercise is not to be the voice of gloom, but now and then it helps to give yourself a wake-up call. You *won't* live forever—so what will you choose to spend your precious energy on *while you're here?*

When you force yourself to look at it that way, taking control of where every moment of your day is spent gets easier. Your energy is much too important to waste on those activities and people and directions that don't lead you where you want to go.

WHERE WILL YOU GO FROM HERE?

The best way to preserve your energy and get more

enthusiasm is to make sure you're in the right place in your life and doing the right things with the time you've been given.

If you're not certain what those things are, listen to yourself. Your programs will give you a clue.

Anytime you catch yourself repeatedly saying, *"I'm tired,"* or *"I just don't have the energy,"* or similar kinds of program statements, *stop and look at what you're doing.* Unless you're physically in the middle of running a marathon, if you're constantly tired, you're probably putting your energy in the wrong place.

The reverse is also true. Pay attention to those times when you say, *"I feel great!"* Whatever you're doing at the time is probably something that *builds* your energy instead of tearing it down.

The rest is simple: do more of the second, and less of the first. Your energy and enthusiasm will increase, your self-esteem will go up, and your life will get better as a result.

I know that could sound like a solution that's almost *too* simple. But ask someone who has a lot of energy, and she'll tell you that it's true.

Now we're going to look at specific programs you can use to help you determine how you want to spend your priceless remaining time and energy. So far, I've shown you how programming works, and given you new Self-Talk programs in each of the major areas of *who you are.* In this next section, I'm going to cover the programs about *what you do.*

Part III
Your Programs
About What You Do

How much time
do you spend
doing things
that don't matter?

It's your _life_.
What are you doing with it?

Chapter 14

WHAT ARE YOU DOING?

*T*he first six Self-Talk scripts deal with the "internal" you, the person you are on the inside. These next six scripts deal with the "external" you, the activities and actions you undertake in the course of a day.

REMEMBER THE VOTE

It is in this next area of programs that the "voting" process explained earlier becomes especially important. This is where you will make actual realistic changes in your *habits*. These are the programs that will help you get to work on time, put money in the bank, express yourself clearly, work through the challenges that confront you, do well in your job or career, and reach the goals you set.

As you read, you should begin to get an idea of how having the right *programs* can help you take the right *actions*. No one expects you to miraculously be able to do everything perfectly right away, just because you've read this book and understand Self-Talk and reprogramming. But even the simple step of being *aware* of the power your programs have to affect your actions can dramatically impact what you do next.

SETTING UP THE PATTERN
FOR YOUR FUTURE

As I mentioned earlier, in Chapter 21 we'll be going over a specific series of steps you can follow to begin taking action to change your programs for good. For now, the goal is to give you a clear script of Self-Talk for each area of programs, and to give you an idea of some of the changes that can happen in each area of your life when you have the right programs on your side.

Reading the Self-Talk scripts can help, even if you only read them once—but keep in mind that *repetition* is the key. At this stage, you should already be working to eliminate negative input, and you should have a clear picture of the difference between a helpful program and a harmful one.

By reading each script and thinking about its impact on your everyday life, you're getting ready to put your new knowledge to work for you. When you reach the action steps and begin practicing what you have learned, you'll be very familiar with what your new programs in each area should look and sound like.

This part of the process is where you start to set up the *pattern* for your new Self-Talk program highways to follow. For each program area, you're making those first faint impressions in your mind that, through repetition, will soon become a path, then a road, then a superhighway that leads to the attitudes and the actions which will drive your future.

So you can set and follow the right direction as you build your new set of practical, action-oriented programs, let's focus on the way you choose your direction in the first place. It's time to take a look at your *goals*.

Believe in your dreams,
believe in your goals,
and believe in yourself.

Every day that goes by
will bring you closer
to reaching your dreams
and making them
come true
in your life.

Your goals
are the pathway
to your dreams.

Chapter 15

SELF-TALK FOR
SETTING GOALS

$\mathcal{A}$lmost no one sets goals! That is, actual, thought-out, written-down kinds of goals. And of the few people who *do* think about and write down goals on a regular basis, few of *them* are women.

If you set goals and write them down, you get where you're going—better, easier and faster than if you don't. If you're already a woman who recognizes the power of setting clear, solid goals, you know what I'm talking about. If you're not, you're in for a wonderful surprise when you begin to do this.

Unfortunately, setting and reaching goals is not typically taught in the classroom, and most of us reach adulthood before we have any idea what the goal-setting process is all about.

I was in my late twenties before I began to understand the incredible power that lay within the seemingly simple process of identifying my goals and following a simple sequence of action steps to reach them. Once I knew how it worked, I wished someone had told me about it sooner!

What I discovered was this: *whatever* it is you want to accomplish, *wherever* it is you want to go, *whoever* it is you want to become—having a *goal* can make all of these things happen. Many people, however, especially women, are forced to struggle and work harder than they have to, simply because no one told them the truth about goals, or took the time to show them how it worked.

In writing this book, I did an informal survey of everyone I knew, asking each of them the same two questions. Whether I was talking to a man or a woman, I asked, "How many of the women you know set goals and review them on a regular basis?" I then asked, "How many of the men you know set goals and review them regularly?"

Even though I am acquainted with many successful individuals, the answers from each person showed that a surprisingly low number of people set goals. And every time, the number of *women* who practiced the process of goal-setting was much lower than the number of *men* who did so.

I realize my study was far from scientific, and yet the results were conclusive: more men than women set goals, and use them to get what they want out of life.

GOALS AREN'T JUST FOR GUYS

If you are a woman who sets goals, as I am, this news may distress you. I didn't want to believe it, at first. But once I realized it was true, I decided to do everything in my power to share what I know about goals with other women.

It's not necessary to be a working professional, or a go-for-it achiever type, to benefit from learning how to use goals to get more of what you want out of life. The same process applies to literally any area of your life, from deciding to go back to school and get a degree to raising good and healthy kids, from being the top sales person in your region to starting and succeeding in your own business, or simply being able to set aside a few hours a day or a week just for you.

The difference between having what you want out of life and not having it is the difference between just having *dreams* and having a specific *goal plan* to make your dreams a reality.

THE DIFFERENCE BETWEEN
"*I WISH*" AND "*I CHOOSE*"

There is a world of difference between the accidental, hopeful way many women live their lives, and the deliberate, confident way followed by women who set real goals. The difference is clearly shown in the words they use.

If you follow the average woman around for a day or a week, and take notes about everything she says, you'll hear her say things like:

178

I <u>wish</u> I could do that, but . . .
I'd like to . . .
Someday I'll . . .
I just don't think I . . .

If you follow a goal-setter around for a similar period of time, your notes will be quite different. You'll probably hear sentences that begin with the following kinds of words:

I choose to . . .
I'm working on . . .
I am . . .
I have . . .

Look at the difference! On the surface, both women want similar things, but their words reveal that they have radically different mental programs underneath.

WHAT CAN *YOU* DO WHEN YOU COMBINE PROGRAMMING WITH THE POWER OF GOALS?

Unless you already have everything you want out of life, making the decision to set some goals will improve your overall situation.

The goal-setting process has specific steps. But before you get to the part where you roll up your sleeves and actually begin to construct your goal list, let's make sure you have the right programs about goals.

As you read the following Self-Talk, picture yourself becoming more like the person this script describes. Don't worry if how you feel about yourself now is nothing like what you're hearing. When you trade in your old programs for the right new Self-Talk programs, and add the right action plan, you will get there.

Self-Talk for Setting Goals

I set goals, and I reach them.

I know that I can have more of what I want in my life by setting a goal, making a plan, and taking action every day.

I never fear failure, and I never fear success.

I'm up to it. I've got what it takes to succeed and achieve, and I know I can.

I believe in my dreams, I believe in my goals, and I believe in myself.

When I set a goal, I make sure it represents the very best of me. I am a quality person, and my goals show it.

I really like setting goals!

Everything I do, everything I say, and everywhere I go, I keep my most important goals in mind. I keep myself focused, so I can stay on the right path.

180

Every day that goes by brings me closer to reaching my dreams and making them come true in my life.

My life is better because I set goals.

I know who I am, I know where I'm going, and I know what it takes to get there.

With each good goal I reach, I feel myself getting stronger, more on track, and more in control of my life.

I never forget that my goals are the pathways to my dreams—and I know I can get there.

Whenever I feel unsure of what to do next, I make a plan, and write down the small steps I need to take to reach the larger objective. Then, I take the first step.

I destroy doubt with the words, "I can do this! And I know I can."

I set great goals, I take positive action, and I absolutely, positively refuse to give up. I am a winner, because I set goals!

That may not sound like you yet, but it will, if you put the right mental programs in place to make it true about you.

HOW TO SET
AND REACH YOUR GOALS

Setting and reaching goals is a simple process, but it can make a powerful difference in your life. If you already set goals, use this as a review; if not, this will teach you the basics:

1. Decide what you want. Wave your wand. A goal can be anything you want, as simple as saving enough money every month to go out to dinner, or as complicated as completing a college degree. Dream as big as you can, and don't limit yourself in advance.

2. Write it down. Surprisingly, even though this step is incredibly easy, *this is the one most people skip*. Don't skip it. Write each goal down on paper, in clear and definite words, *exactly* as you want it to happen. Be specific. It's also a good idea to use visual reminders of your goals such as photos, drawings, blueprints, and even pictures cut from magazines. Put them where you can see them; surround yourself with clear pictures of what you want.

3. List the action steps required to achieve the goal. Any task, no matter how large it seems at first, can be broken down into a series of steps. For each of your goals, start at the beginning, write down the first step, and continue listing the steps until you reach the end. If you have trouble figuring out the first step, it sometimes helps to work backward from your goal until your list of action steps is clear and complete.

4. Prioritize your goals—choose a goal to work on. You can begin in two ways. You can choose to start with something small in order to get used to reaching your goals. That's always a good idea, because it builds confidence and puts programs in place that show you what you can accomplish. Or, you can start with your most important goal, even if it's a major target with many action steps.

5. Take the first action step. You'll be surprised how easy this is once you've identified what the steps are. Whatever the first step is, *just do it.* Don't worry about making a mistake. If you don't like the results, you get to change them.

6. Repeat #5 until you reach the final step. Keep doing it. Put one foot in front of the other, and take one step at a time until you accomplish your goal. While you're at it, keep your goal sheet handy and read it often, every day if you can. Reading your goals and action steps is critical, especially when you're new to the process.

7. Reward yourself. Too many women leave out this part. They either think reaching the goal is reward enough, or they don't believe they deserve the reward in the first place. This is a good time to break that habit, and build some new programs about deserving to succeed. Your reward could be as simple as taking yourself out to lunch, or as major as taking a vacation. It's impossible to put too much time and effort into finding out which rewards motivate you most. Do you enjoy quiet time with friends? A new box of stationery—or a special box of chocolates? A private date with your husband? Choose a reward that is in line with the size of the achievement, accept the reward, and be proud of what you've done.

8. Read your list again, and choose another goal to work on. Follow it through the action steps all the way to the goal achievement and the reward. Before long, you'll be able to tackle more than one goal at a time. The more you practice setting and reaching goals, the better you'll be at it.

9. Review and reevaluate your list every 30 days. This doesn't mean you should only *read* your goals once a month. You should work at building the habit of reading your goals often; daily is best. I'm talking here about a monthly evaluation of your desires and direction.

Even after practicing goal-setting for years, I still have a monthly goal review. I especially like to work on setting my goals just after I've had a birthday. It's much easier to deal with being another year older when I can see what I've accomplished in that year.

10. Give yourself strong new programs of setting and reaching goals. This step is critical. I didn't get good at the goal-setting process until I put the right new programs in place. I chose to listen to the professional Self-Talk cassettes available on the subject of setting and reaching goals because I don't have a lot of free time, and I knew from experience that the tapes worked best.

By the way, I'm *delighted* to tell you that I finally reached one of my own major long-term goals: for the first time ever, Self-Talk Cassettes featuring the scripts of Self-Talk for women are now available in a *woman's* voice. (All the scripts from this book are available on professionally prerecorded cassettes, and I've included the tape publisher's name and address in the back of the book for your convenience.)

It's no surprise to me that the tape script on goals is one of the most popular. It works, and the proof that it works is the book you're holding in your hands.

WHAT SELF-TALK FOR SETTING GOALS HAS DONE FOR ME

People often ask me when and how I decided to be a writer. The truth is that I can't remember a time in my life when I *didn't* want to write. When I was a child, my family lived next door to the public library, and when I was 5 I became the youngest person in my town to ever have her own library card. My mother got tired of taking me to exchange books, because I was a voracious reader.

I quickly worked my way through all the Nancy Drew books (which, by the way, are *full* of positive program images of girls being self-sufficient and successful), and then graduated to classics and the great writers of American fiction. I've heard good writing described as a conversation between the writer and the reader, and my "talks" with people like John Steinbeck, Walt Whitman, and Ernest Hemingway have added many wonderful hours to my life.

As an adult, no matter where I went or what I did, my desire to write remained strong. My dream was to someday write the great American novel—but I knew very little about how one actually goes about doing that.

When I learned about Self-Talk, and then about how to

use Self-Talk to set and reach goals, something "clicked" inside me. "Aha!" I thought. "So *that's* how it's done!"

I put the goal-setting process to the test. I set a concrete and specific goal to complete the novel and to see it published, then gave myself strong and repeated Self-Talk programs that told me I reach the goals I set. In that process, I learned that I would much rather write a book that is fun, interesting, suspenseful to read and popular, than a great work of literature that would be read and appreciated by only a few.

I got the new programs I needed, and I reached my goal. My first novel is now a reality. It is called *The Quarry*, and it is the story of a church bus of children on their way to camp one rainy Saturday morning . . . that never arrives at its destination. I won't tell you who took the children and why, or what happens next—but I can say I had a great time writing the book, and I already know how the second novel (featuring the same main character) turns out.

I not only completed the novel I had always wanted to write, but I also used the same process to write *this* book.

When I've reached my *next* writing goal, you'll know— because you'll see my books on the bestseller list.

Before I discovered how to apply Self-Talk to help me reach my goals, I would never have dared to make such a bold and public statement of my dreams. But now I know how it works. Because of Self-Talk and my new programs, *I reach my goals*—and no matter what *your* goals and dreams are, the same can become true for you.

WHAT KIND OF GOALS WILL YOU CHOOSE?

What would you like to see on *your* list? Have you ever taken the time to find out? This would be a great time to stop *wishing*, and start getting the job done—because your old *wish* list will now be a *goal* list instead. Now that you've started learning the right positive programs of Self-Talk, and are familiar with a step-by-step process to help you, you will find it much easier to *identify*—and *reach*—your goals.

Because you are organized,
you know which direction
you want to go.

Because you know your goals,
you know the steps to take
to get there.

Because you believe in yourself,
you will never stop.

Chapter 16

SELF-TALK FOR
PERSONAL ORGANIZATION

*O*etails, details, details. Life is full of them. Your old self-talk might even tell you things like *"There are a thousand and one things to get done in a day, and a thousand and two reasons why I can never catch up!"* These days, it seems like we're buried in details.

For women, the problem stems from our own desperate insistence to measure up, to do it all, to fill all those different pairs of shoes at once, and to do it better than anyone else we know. Even if you're not a driven over-achiever type, you probably still feel that nagging sense of self-doubt that tells you something, somewhere, has been left undone—and that it's somehow *your* fault!

The demands of balancing home, family, career, fitness, spirituality, romance, and finances allow very little time left over to just be *you*. By now, you may have nearly given up on the notion that you can carve out a space in your day, even a tiny one, just for yourself. To even *think* about such a luxury could make you feel guilty or disloyal to all those people who are counting on you to come through.

But where does it all stop? At what point do we, as women, get to say, "*Hold it*, world, it's time for *me*!"? Is there anything we can do about the pressures of our busy lives, short of trying harder and still harder to bear up under the strain? Shouldn't there be a better way?

There is, and it starts with taking a good hard look at what's truly important to you.

IT STARTS WITH YOUR PRIORITIES

Your first priority should be to figure out who or what is running your life, and make sure *you* have some say in the matter. I'm definitely not telling you that you should suddenly rebel against all forms of authority or to tell your boss, your mother or father, your husband and your kids that they no longer get to place any demands on your time.

None of us lives in a vacuum, and we have all developed personality styles and compromises that allow us to live peaceful lives. The *last* thing I recommend is that you disrupt your life by becoming drastically independent. If you did that, "independent" might equate to "living alone."

Just make sure you remember that this is *your* life, and put your own needs somewhere on your list of things to take care of.

After that first and most significant priority of making sure someone else isn't dictating your choices and actions for you, it's a good idea to figure out which other things are important in your life. What counts most to you, and in what order? Is it your husband and family, your job, your favorite sport, your education, a meaningful hobby, or all of the above?

The goal is to be aware of what is most important to you, so you can allocate the assets of your time and energy accordingly.

DO YOU FOCUS MOST ON WHAT MATTERS LEAST?

How much time do you spend trying to get better at doing things that don't even *matter*? How many of the details of your day could you take off your list without making much of an impact on your life? And what is your life *about* in the first place—what is all this organizing really for?

If you want to be more organized, and be able to get more done, remember that the goal should be to make your life *easier* day by day, *not* harder or more complicated.

Where does your energy go? Do you put the most time and effort into the areas at the top of your priority list, or do you spend those limited resources on getting things done that really don't add to your life in a meaningful way?

If you're feeling the pressure to be more organized for

the wrong reasons, you might want to rethink your priorities. If you're listening to the wrong voice telling you what to do and who to be, or if you're majoring in minor things instead of the important ones, getting more organized will *not* automatically improve your life!

However, if you *are* already setting your direction for yourself, and you *do* already have your priorities straight, but you are still feeling overloaded, there are some things you can do that can help you solve that problem.

A LIST OF QUESTIONS THAT CAN HELP

When you're feeling overwhelmed and disorganized, it helps to give yourself a clear picture of what exactly is *causing* your disorganization. This can be difficult to do when you're right in the middle of chaos.

This short list of questions can help you make sense of the confusion created when you have too much to do and not enough time or not enough of the right skills to handle everything on your list.

1. What can you take off your list? First, *make the list. Write everything down* that you feel you ought to get done, no matter how long the list is. Then, cross off any items you can see that clearly are not important, even if it's only one or two items.

Most of us are good at making lists of things to do, thinking it will make us more organized. This question will show you the value of deciding what *not* to do.

2. Are your priorities straight? Which items are most important to *you*, and why? Which ones don't count as much? Write your list again, in priority order from most important to least important, and as you do, see if anything at the bottom of the list can be deleted.

I learned how quickly I could live with not getting everything done when I was living in our 200-year-old Colonial farmhouse while it was being restored. There is nothing like a major remodeling project to teach you how impossible it can be to "catch up" on the details of things to do.

I'm the kind of woman who likes to get the laundry clean, folded, and put away on the same day—preferably with no single socks left over when I'm done. By the time the house was finished, I had learned to settle for *finding* the washer and dryer, much less finding the dirty clothes! Sometimes I'd give up, go outside, and spend time pruning my antique roses, just to get *something* done.

The house is beautiful now, and I have rematched all my socks and put them away—but the lesson stayed with me. I'm much less hard on myself now if every little thing doesn't get done the way I'd like. I can even skip the laundry on purpose now and then, and the rose garden and my disposition are better for it.

3. Who can you get to help you? Now that you know what you need to do most, what can you delegate?

A good way to unclutter your list is to figure out which tasks you enjoy or are good at, then trade tasks with your friends, neighbors, and family members. Do you like to cook, and hate to put gas in the car or take it to change the oil? Make a double recipe of a casserole for dinner, and "pay" your brother to get the car serviced for you by sharing your home-cooked meal.

I've learned it's a lot more fun, for instance, to clean someone else's kitchen and bathrooms than it is to do my own. When I was working and going to school, I had several friends who felt the same way, so we would swap. It helped.

Is paperwork something you're good at? Arrange to reorganize a friend's office in return for her watering your plants or feeding your pets for a week. Even a brief "vacation" from the repetitious everyday tasks can leave you feeling much more in control.

Look around you. See your life in a different light, and figure out which items on your list need your personal touch, and which ones can do without it.

4. Which area gives you the most headaches? Is it paperwork? Mail? Laundry? Dishes? Running errands? If you can identify your biggest problem areas, it will help you figure out where to put your energy in order to move forward. If you can gain control of even one of your toughest trouble spots, that sense of accomplishment will spill over into the other areas as well.

5. Are you trying to do the impossible? I can't begin to count the hours of time I've wasted in my life trying to organize tasks that are chaotic by nature.

It's a difficult fact of life that some people, and some situations, are going to be messy and chaotic *no matter what you do!* If you're trying to fix the unfixable, you might want to refocus that same energy on other areas that you can do something about.

6. Are you focused on your goals? If you're feeling disorganized and out of control, the best way I know to fix that feeling fast is for you to reread your goal list. When you do, you'll find that even tasks that make you feel like you're spinning your wheels at the time *are actually moving you forward toward one of your goals.* Frequently reading your goals helps you monitor your progress and lets you see whether your priorities are in the right order. The more often you focus on your goals, the more organized and in control you will become.

7. What's the worst that can happen if you don't get it all done? Before you go off the deep end on this one and start imagining all sorts of terrible things, stop a moment. Remember to be realistic. Who will really *care* if all your socks don't get folded, or even if you don't get them all clean at once? What harm will it do if you bring a store-bought pie to your mom's for Thanksgiving dinner, just this once? Will anyone notice, or care? And do you care if they do, enough to spend your precious energy on that particular task?

If you can, skip it. Let it go, so you can focus on those tasks that really *matter* to you and the people you care about.

8. When is the last time you gave yourself a break? Are you being too hard on yourself? Lighten up, and relax!

How long has it been since you took five minutes or ten, or an hour, for yourself? *Give yourself a break.* Ease up. Go for a walk, with or without the dog. Buy yourself an ice cream cone, and take the time to sit down in a pleasant place and eat it—*not* in the car on your way

195

home.

Take time out, and when you get back, you'll be able to get more done in less time than you could before.

9. Do you have the right mental programs in place about personal organization? The other items on this list can help you regain control of your day, but unless you fix the mental programs that caused the disorganization in the first place, you'll have, at best, only a temporary solution. The *only* way to get organized and stay that way is to give yourself strong new programs which tell you that *being in control of your life* is the way you *are*.

I recommend you keep this list of questions handy, to read anytime you feel like you're so far behind you'll never catch up. I keep everything like that in the same notebook with my to-do list and my goal sheet. It helps me organize my thoughts, and while I'm organizing, I save time by having it all in one place.

SELF-TALK FOR
PERSONAL ORGANIZATION

Here's a script of new Self-Talk programs to help you make those organized habits a permanent part of you. Remember, the rest of the steps are useless without the following kinds of personal programs working for you every minute.

196

Self-Talk for Personal Organization

My mind is in order, and so is my life.

I am always on track, because I have given myself the right new mental programs that get me organized and keep me that way.

I have learned the skills of managing my time, setting goals, and taking personal responsibility for my life. I do what I need to do, on time and in the right way.

I really like being in control. I continually work to improve my attitude and my mental posture, and it shows in the way I manage my physical environment.

I choose to be neat, clean, and orderly in all that I do. I feel better about myself when I take charge of the details of my life.

When I find myself feeling overwhelmed by my day-to-day responsibilities, I stop, step back, and refocus on my long-term goals. I keep my perspective, and I keep my balance.

If I need help, I say so. If I don't know how to do something, I find out. If I don't know the answer, I admit it. That's how I learn; that's how I grow.

I never put myself down for the way I manage my life. If everything isn't exactly the way I want it to be, I just keep believing in my ability to make it better.

My priorities are straight. I know that people are usually more important than paperwork. I set high standards and work to achieve them, but I always remember to smile while I strive for success.

I create peace of mind by the order of my surroundings. My life is clean, my heart is right, and I do everything it takes to keep it that way.

I respect myself, and I respect others. I treat their time as carefully as I treat my own, and I make sure not to waste a moment of it.

I keep my goals in front of me, so I never forget the things that really matter in my life.

No matter how busy I am, I take time for myself. I protect my energy, and apply it to reaching my dreams.

I look for and find positive role models who live their lives in an organized and successful way. I watch what they do, I think about what they have achieved, and I follow their lead.

I take advantage of the tools of success that teach me how to live a better life. I read, I study, I practice, and I get more organized with every step I take.

If I make a mistake, I don't dwell on what I did wrong. I figure it out, I learn from it, and I move on.

I enjoy being organized! The more I work at it, the easier it gets.

Because I am organized, I know what direction I want to go. Because I know my goals, I know the steps to take to get there. Because I believe in myself, I will never stop.

With that kind of Self-Talk programs automatically and naturally helping you organize your day, you will be able to do more of the things that matter to you and let go more easily of the things that don't. You'll see your goals more clearly and be able to reach them more efficiently, because you'll be putting your energy in the right places.

Whatever your work
happens to be,
the right Self-Talk programs
can make it better.

The key is to make sure
the work you do
is in alignment
with your goals,
and will help you take
your life
in the direction
you want it to go.

Chapter 17

SELF-TALK FOR
THE WORK YOU DO

*N*o matter what work you do, you can benefit from having the right programs of Self-Talk to help you do it better. Whether you are a full-time working woman, a stay-at-home mom or wife, a volunteer worker, someone who devotes time to charity work, or half of a two-income family, the work you do is important to you.

The same set of rules applies to anything you do, whether you want to improve your skills, your potential, or your attitude.

The following Self-Talk is designed to help you build on the best of the mental programs you already have about your work, and strengthen your program paths in areas where you might not be as strong or as confident as you would like to be.

Remember, each of the Self-Talk scripts in this book is

here as a guideline, to set up a pattern for your own programs to follow. We'll get down to specific application techniques later. For now, if you want to be more successful at the work you do, this kind of Self-Talk will help you make it happen.

As you read the following words, picture yourself going about your typical day. But this time, picture how your day would go if you had these positive mental programs on your side.

Self-Talk for The Work You Do

I choose to enjoy the work I do each day.

I never allow the challenges or requirements of my job to affect my attitude in a negative way. I stay up, positive, and on track—no matter what!

I always remember that others are observing me as I do my job, so I make it a point to show them the very best I have to offer.

I know where I'm going, and I know what it will take to get me there.

I have strong goals, and my work moves me closer to reaching them every day.

I keep my eyes and ears open for new ways to do my job even better. If I find a better way, I put it into practice immediately.

I always make sure the work I choose is helping my life and my goals in the most positive way.

Other people admire me for the way I do my job. I set a positive example in everything I do.

I treat everyone with respect, regardless of their level. Whether I work for them or they work for me, I make sure we work together.

I see competition as a healthy way to improve myself and my performance, and I always do my best.

I never put someone else down to make myself look good. I stand on my own achievements, and I come out on top.

If someone has a problem with me or my work, I never put off correcting the situation. I tackle it directly, and immediately, and I get it fixed.

I am always preparing for my next level, instead of getting comfortable where I am. I like moving forward, and I am!

I make sure I am rewarded for my time and talents in a way that matches my attitude and ability. I get what I deserve.

I choose to do work that benefits me and those I love. My work fits my plan, both for now and for later.

I see my work as a powerful, rewarding part of my life.

I never fail to give my best effort, and because I am willing to work hard, I am moving up, moving out and moving on.

Does that sound like you? It *is* you, the person you can be with the right programs in place about your work.

WHAT IF YOUR WORK ISN'T WORKING FOR YOU?

The goal of this chapter is to provide you with the mental programs you need to make every moment of your work day go more smoothly. But what if your working life is a struggle, and it seems like there is no end in sight and no hope of it ever getting better?

It might help to know you're not alone in your feelings of frustration, anger, helplessness, or even despair. We've all had times in our lives when we were dissatisfied with our work, and wished we could just quit.

The worst job I ever had was when I was in college, working as a film projectionist as part of a work-study financial aid package. In return for finding me a job on campus, the university got the benefit of twenty hours a week of my time at four dollars an hour.

It was the hardest eighty dollars a week I've ever earned. I suffered through hours of painstaking film repair work on the movies the students were required to watch as part of their classwork, splicing and gluing together fragments of old film that was long past its useful life span.

I sat for four hours a day at a huge machine that spun the film from one reel to the other at high speed. The machine was *supposed* to stop automatically when it sensed a break or a trouble spot in the film, but it seldom worked that way. What *usually* happened is that the machine would keep spinning the reels in spite of the broken film, which meant that the film would go wild, spitting yards and yards of it in impossible tangles all over me, the machine, the floor, and the film library room.

The most difficult part wasn't creating order out of the chaos the machine caused, although that was a mess. It was the constant tension of never knowing *when* disaster would strike, followed by the repeated shocks to my nervous system each time the film broke again—which it inevitably did, several times a day.

I needed the job and the money, though, so I hung in there—until something *else* happened that convinced me once and for all that I had to find something else to do.

JOHN STEINBECK, I'M SORRY

The regular projectionist got sick, so I was asked to go to the university theater and run the projector. The first three evenings went all right. I've always liked John Steinbeck, and I didn't really mind seeing *The Grapes of Wrath* six times in three days. But on the fourth night, something went wrong with one of the projectors.

When it came time for a reel change, the projectors were *supposed* to switch automatically from one to the other. The projector for the new reel would turn on, the old one would shut off, and the show would go on.

On the second reel of *The Grapes of Wrath*, the projector for the new reel got stuck. The high-intensity lamp came on, but the reel didn't move. Forty jeering college students watched in glee, and I watched in horror, as Henry Fonda's earnest face on film began to bubble, then smoke, then *melt* as the heat from the lamp cooked the motionless film.

It happened over, and over, and over. By the time I gave up on the new projector and switched the reel to the old one, I was exhausted, in tears, and absolutely determined that I would never go through a nightmare like that again as long as I lived.

I quit the next day.

CAN YOU CHANGE YOUR CHOICE?

If you are currently working in an area that is not well-suited to your skills, your goals, and your overall direction in life, it's no surprise that you're less than enthusiastic where your work is concerned.

If that sounds like you, you have two options. Either you can *change* what you do, or you *can't*. We're going to look at each of those two scenarios one at a time, starting with what you can do if you feel you are unwilling or unable to change the work you do.

The second scenario could sound negative or defeatist, considering that this is a book designed to get you to see your life as one that is full of unlimited potential. And it's true that I want to encourage you in every way I can to live out the very best your life has to offer.

But no matter how badly you want to leave your current circumstances and go do something else, that's often an unrealistic expectation. When you have bills to pay and others are counting on you to earn an income, you may not be able to change your job, at least not *yet*.

If you are at a time in your life when your work just isn't working for you, there are some things you can do, beginning immediately, to improve your situation.

IF YOU'RE STAYING WHERE YOU ARE, YOU CAN STILL MAKE IT BETTER

I'm by no means suggesting you should give up and accept your circumstances as the best you can do. But until and unless you can figure out a way to free yourself from your current job, the time you spend there is a big part of your life. An attitude change on your part can go a long way toward improving how you feel about every moment of your working day.

If you are in a job or on a career path that is not likely to change in the near future, but you're not happy with it, I have a few suggestions that might help. Feel free to pick and choose from the list at random, and try as many of the ideas as you'd like.

If you want to feel better about your work, you can:

o   **Make a list of what you like about the work you do.** Read it anytime you start to wish you were somewhere else.

207

o   **Find someone else who does the same work, and loves it.** Talk to that person about what she likes most about her work.

o   **Avoid complainers.** Negativity rubs off, and if you are already less than happy about your job, it won't do you any good to commiserate with someone else who feels the same way.

o   **Read your goal list, and find ways in which your work is helping you reach your goals.** It's a lot easier to put up with even a long-term work situation that is less than ideal, if you can see that it will eventually help you achieve your goals.

o   **Look for ways to improve your current situation.** Almost any circumstance has potential for improvement, if you look at it with the expectation of finding ways to make it better.

o   **Identify what it is about your particular work you dislike most.** If there is a particular area or task that repeatedly causes you stress, see if there is a way to work around it. Sometimes, if you solve the small problems that irritate you the most, the overall picture can seem much brighter.

o   **Give yourself plenty of upbeat, positive programs about the work you do.** Listen to a Self-Talk tape on the way to work, around the house as you do the chores, or even at the office, if you can. Whenever negativity rears its head, you'll have the right programs to help you get rid of it immediately.

o **Count your blessings.** You've heard it before, many times. There's a reason for that: it works. No matter how bad off you believe you are, there's always someone who would trade with you in an instant if she had the chance. If you don't feel blessed, take a good look around you. It won't take long for you to find someone less fortunate than you are. Even if your situation isn't perfect, you can always choose to be thankful for what you have.

WHAT IF IT'S TIME
TO MOVE ON?

If you've tried everything and nothing works, if you've simply decided it's time to make a change in the work you do, the right attitude can make the process easier. If you're not sure *what* you want to do but you know you want something different, here are some reminders you can fall back on when you need positive encouragement:

o **Don't underestimate yourself.** You have talents, skills, and abilities you may not even know about yet. If you don't have the skills you need, you can learn them; if you don't know the people who can help you achieve your new direction, you can meet them; if you don't have the mental programs that let you see yourself being successful, you can change them.

○ **If you want to progress, you can find someone to help you.** I have yet to meet a woman who wanted to improve herself and her life, who could not find a positive support system of friends and mentors to help her do so. If you're married, start with your husband. Any positive change you make will also improve his life, as long as you always make sure that his goals and your joint goals will be met in the process. Your kids can also be a surprising source of love, support and encouragement.

○ **Remember that your ultimate security is up to you.** Too many women stay in a dead-end job because they feel it offers them "security." These days, the truth behind the myth is easy to see. Just because you work for a large company doesn't mean it can't downsize; just because you're good at your job doesn't mean you can't one day be laid off. If you have the right kind of healthy confidence and faith in your own abilities, you will have the beginnings of *true* security.

○ **You always have a choice.** One of the most difficult and frightening aspects of making a change in the work you do is the realization that what you decide to do with your life is, in large part, up to *you* to figure out. If you feel stuck, go back to your goal list, pray about it, talk it over with your mate, your family, your best friend, or all of them, and *decide*. If your choice doesn't work out, you can always make another—and you'll almost certainly grow in the process.

o **You have the ability to give yourself new programs of confidence and self-belief.** Use the Self-Talk that shows you the best picture of yourself meeting challenges and loving it. Also, go back to the chapter on self-esteem and reread it for a week or two. One of the best times to give yourself strong new programs is when you're considering a change in your work, because the right Self-Talk can help you focus on who you are and what you really want from your life.

o **You can keep the good, and leave the rest.** In any situation, even one that didn't work out for the best, there is something of value to be gained from the experience. Rather than being bitter and focusing on old negative mental pathways of doubt and failure, you can choose instead to concentrate on what you learned in the process. Even if you can't yet see the value of that particular experience, every forward step you take makes you stronger and better able to deal with the new challenges that will come with your change of direction.

Whether you continue your current work or decide to do something new, the key in both cases is to do your best to make sure that the work you do will lead your life in the direction you ultimately want it to go.

If you keep your goals firmly in mind, review them often, and make sure you add the right new programs to help you stay on track with your dreams, your work can be intensely satisfying and rewarding.

Your wishes
are essential.

It is what you say
right after the words,
"I wish . . ."
that is the expression
of your dreams.

Listen carefully.

Chapter 18

Self-Talk for Money and Finances

*W*hat are your programs about money, and what do they say about you? Do you see yourself as a person for whom having money is no problem, or is it easier to believe having enough will always be a struggle?

There are few words in the language that can open more mental file drawers at high speed than that single word, "money." Our views about money, and having it or not, are inseparably woven into our pictures of our past, our beliefs about our current life, and our beliefs about what kind of future it is possible for us to have.

Before we move to the new script of Self-Talk about your money and finances, let's examine what some of your old programs about money, or the *lack* of it, might sound like. Here's a short list of the kinds of things people say about money:

I wish we had more money, but . . .
Someday it will be different.
It costs too much.
There's never enough left over at the end of the month.
A day late and a dollar short . . .
We can't afford it.
It seems like we can never get ahead.
I'll always be broke.
Someday my ship will come in.
When I win the lottery, I'll . . .
Money can't buy happiness.
Rich people are selfish.
Money is the root of all evil.

As you read that list, you'll notice several specific types of financial attitudes, including hopefulness, resignation, dreaming or being unrealistic, and even anger.

Let's break down those programs and take a look at what they're really saying. The specific words of the programs provide us with the clues that tell us how to fix the problem.

STOP *HOPING,* AND START MAKING IT

1. The "I Hope" Mentality

The first type of attitude is the *"I hope"* mentality. This is the person who is *wishful.* People who are unrealistic about their finances use words like "I wish," "I hope," "someday," and "maybe," to describe their own beliefs about their potential to have money.

Wishes aren't bad; they are essential. It is what you say right after the words "I wish" that expresses your dreams, and it pays to listen carefully. The key here is to turn your *wishes* about money into programmed *goals* about money.

You can still be practical and realistic, but it's surprising how many dreams can become reality when you put the right goals and action steps into motion, along with strong new programs about making money and keeping it.

When you set your money goals, make them realistic and specific. Don't shoot for the moon right at first; gradually progress from a little to a lot. But don't self-limit your financial future by setting your sights too low, either. Set your goal a little bit higher than you think you can reach—and then, *reach*. That's the whole idea of a goal, to show you that you can do more than you currently believe you can.

As you work on your Self-Talk and begin to reach your first goal levels of your finances, you start to build even more positive programs of belief in your own ability to be financially strong.

IT DOESN'T HAVE TO BE THIS WAY, JUST BECAUSE THAT'S HOW IT'S ALWAYS BEEN

2. The "Bystander" Mentality

At a certain point in their lives, women who have never had success with money stop believing they ever will.

They give up, give in, and give out. They become resigned to what they think is their fate, believing it will never change.

When that happens, they have fallen into the second type of attitude about having money: the *"Bystander"* mentality. This is the kind of woman who feels *powerless* to affect the state of her own finances. She believes that nothing she does will make any difference anyway, so why try?

Most of these women, if asked, would probably tell you they believe it's much easier for a man to make a lot of money or to be wealthy than it is for a woman to do the same thing. They think that's how it's always been, that's how it will always be for them, and there's no way for them to change it.

IT'S NOT WHO YOU ARE— IT'S WHAT *PROGRAMS* YOU HAVE

Those "bystanders," those women who feel powerless to make a financial difference in their own lives, forget about one thing, or never learned it in the first place: *Any woman can have plenty of money, if her own mental programs about money tell her she can.*

It doesn't make any difference how old you are, how well or poorly you've dealt with your finances in the past, or even how much you currently owe. If you give yourself the right new mental programs that let you see yourself as a person *with* money instead of a person *without* it, your financial picture has no choice but to improve.

That's how it works. I've known women who were broke their whole lives, who learned about the process of reprogramming with Self-Talk, and used what they learned to turn their lives around. I've seen dramatic financial improvements in a remarkably short time after those women got off their old mental highways that led to failure instead of success.

If you're a bystander, you need to work on your programs of self-belief and self-esteem, along with programs about taking action and moving forward. It's a good idea to also focus on programs of energy and enthusiasm, so you'll have the mental fuel to get you where you're going.

IF YOUR SHIP HASN'T COME IN, START SWIMMING

3. The "Lottery Winner" Mentality

The third type of financial attitude many women have is the "*Lottery Winner*" mentality. These women fall into the trap of thinking a grand event like the lottery or some person *out there* is going to miraculously rescue them from their financial pit.

Just as the word *wishful* applies to the "*I Hope*" mentality, and the word *powerless* applies to the "*Bystander*" mind set, there is an adjective for this one as well. The word is *dreaming,* and for a change, I'm not using the word in its positive meaning.

If you're still waiting for some grand event or for

someone *else* to drastically change *your* financial future, *wake up*! Your finances are your *own* responsibility. The only way to be truly financially successful is to accept that responsibility and take control of your finances yourself.

If you have old programs that are telling you you're not responsible for your financial well-being, or that you're not up to the task of doing what needs to be done to create wealth and security, *change the programs.*

If you're *dreaming* about your financial future instead of *working* to build it, take a good, hard look at your programs of personal responsibility, as well as your programs on deserving to succeed. Then get out your goal list and get down to it.

You can do that. You're worth it, and so is your future.

DON'T GET MAD—GET BETTER

4. The "Victim" Mentality

The fourth type of programmed attitude about money that too many women exhibit is a posture of dismay, resentment, and even *anger* at those who seem to be luckier than they are or have more than they do.

I call this the *"Victim"* mentality, and the word that best describes it is feeling *abused.* These are women who believe that the world is somehow unfair, or that there is a force "out there" actively working to hold them down or hold them back. They think someone *else* has all the luck or gets all the breaks where finances are concerned.

The way to defeat that kind of negative thinking is to realize that people who have a lot of money are people just like you. They just have different *programs* about money and finances, and their picture of wealth and success is different from yours.

Your first goal is to change your old programs enough for you to simply be able to see yourself breaking even, while you're building the new programs that allow you to set stronger financial goals.

Start with a plan and an attitude that tells you it is possible for you to get out of debt once and for all. Other people do it every day, and many financial planning experts out there will take you through the process step-by-step—often for free.

Once you've gotten your debt under control and you've started breaking down the old mental highways that have kept you constantly spending more than you make, you can begin to build a financial future that works.

Don't wait until you're out of the hole to decide for yourself how much is enough to make you happy. Again, be realistic, but don't be afraid to stretch. One of the most exciting aspects of reprogramming is what happens when your dreams begin to come alive again. This is different from the unrealistic dreaming of the "*Lottery Winner*" mentality, because this time, it's tied to your *goals* and the *actions* you'll take to reach them.

Don't set your goals too low. As you continue building new program pathways about money, go ahead and type in new instructions to your mental computer that will take you as far financially as you would *really* like to go.

WHEN YOU GAIN MONEY, THAT DOESN'T MEAN YOU LOSE YOURSELF

If you've been programmed to think that "money can't buy happiness," or that "money is the root of all evil," it may be time for a more accurate picture of reality.

To say that money can't buy happiness assumes if you *gain* enough money, you'll automatically have to *lose* those special and important qualities of your life that make you truly rich.

It's just not true to think that if you become financially successful, your values and morals will change, or that the other meaningful areas of your life must suffer as a result.

In my life, gaining financial security has allowed me to care for others and to give of myself and my time in a way I always wanted to do, but could not afford.

WHOEVER YOU ARE,
THAT'S WHO YOU'LL BE

I know many women of great character who are also strong financially. Their happiness stems from the same sources as yours already does: time with their families, satisfying work, fun leisure activities, helping people who need help, and building a life that works.

The biggest difference between them and less successful women is that *they* have been able to let go of the worries that go along with never having enough money, and get on with their lives!

If you've heard, and believed, that "money is the root of all evil," you've probably been a victim of inaccuracy. The actual quote comes from the Biblical book of first Timothy, and it says that the *"love* of money" is the root of evil—*not* the money itself!

That's a major difference. No, money shouldn't be what your life is about, in and of itself—but neither is money a bad thing to have and to use. There are just as many *poor* people who are evil and rotten as there are *rich* people who are bad.

Whatever kind of person you *already* are, that's still how you'll be if you have more money. Keep the mental programs that tell you good things about who you are and what kind of person you are, but also make the choice to change your programs about your finances. If you do, you'll do a lot better. You'll still be *you*—you'll just be you, with more money.

A NEW SET OF PROGRAMS FOR YOUR FINANCIAL FUTURE

This next script of Self-Talk is all about the way you *see* yourself having money. If you're not yet where you want to be financially, these are the kinds of new mental programs that can help you improve your bottom line.

Self-Talk for Financial Freedom

I never forget that success is more than just having money—but I make sure I do everything I need to do to be financially strong.

I have faith that I will always have more than I need.

I enjoy having the money to not only pay for the things I need, but also the things I want.

I am never intimidated by the details of my financial life. I take charge, I take action, and I move forward.

My financial freedom begins with a plan—and I know my plan.

I spend my time with other people who know how to succeed—and I learn from studying what they're doing right.

I deserve to be financially free—and I choose to be.

The work I do every day brings me closer to prosperity. I make sure I'm doing the right things with my time and my energy to build the life I want.

I never listen to those who say it can't be done, or that I haven't got what it takes. I go my own way, because I know I'm right.

I deserve to succeed!

I believe in myself, but I also choose to listen to others who have already been where I want to go. I listen, I learn, I grow, and I prosper because of it.

It doesn't matter to me where I started from. I keep my mind focused on where I'm going.

Having money is a natural and positive part of my life.

I never listen to the opinions of others who try to limit the level of financial success I can reach. I listen to myself, I listen to my goals, and I get where I'm going!

I am never discouraged about money or finances. My positive attitude reduces the challenges and increases my potential for success.

I always remember to reward myself in positive, healthy ways. I stay motivated, and it works!

Money is good to have, and I'm good at having it.

My future is bright, my belief is high, and my goal is in sight. I am thankful for my financial freedom, and I build it every day.

With that kind of Self-Talk as an asset, it won't be long before your own mental programs of financial success take off on their own and start creating the future *you* deserve to have.

When you change your money programs to sound like these, you will join the group of positive women who are financially on track.

IT DOESN'T MATTER
WHERE YOU'RE STARTING FROM

If you feel you can never succeed financially because you're starting from rock-bottom, don't be discouraged.

Many of the most financially secure women started from a background of very difficult circumstances. The key to breaking that old cycle is in creating a positive *new* program cycle about money that will redefine your financial future for you.

Never forget, no matter what your financial status is now, you have at least as good a chance as anyone else who wants to do better financially. And knowing about Self-Talk and programming means you have a better chance than most to succeed.

5. The "Achiever" Mentality

This fifth and final attitude about money is the *"Achiever"* mentality, and the word that sums up that kind of belief is the word *"successful."*

It was a long journey for me from my first job of clearing dirty tables in a restaurant for tips, to my college work-study days at four dollars an hour, to my self-esteem-building military career with a steady salary, and then on to a financially successful speaking and writing career. I had to learn, build, and reinforce an entire new mental pathway of financial strength—and with the right Self-Talk to help me, I eventually got the job done.

Regardless of where you are starting from when it comes to *your* finances, you can improve your financial picture with the right mental programs to help you.

Whether you are now a member of the wishful *"I Hope"* mentality, a *"Bystander"* who feels powerless to change, a dreamer in the *"Lottery Winner"* group, or even one who sees yourself as an abused *"Victim,"* if you do what it takes to give yourself the right powerful new programs about financial freedom, the successful attitude of the *"Achiever"* will soon describe *you*.

If you run into a problem,
worrying about it
doesn't help.

It just burns energy
that would be better spent
figuring out
a solution.

Everyone has problems.

You might as well
get good
at solving them.

Chapter 19

SELF-TALK FOR SOLVING PROBLEMS

*Y*ou may have noticed by now that I believe you should approach *every* situation with a positive, winning attitude. And it's true that I'm a firm believer in expecting the best possible outcome in anything!

But even though it's good to be positive, sometimes when you have a problem, it *isn't* just a "challenge" or an "opportunity for growth." It's a *problem*. And when you have one, your success is going to begin with your programming.

Your attitude can go far toward helping you believe in your own ability to tackle problems and solve them easily. In fact, it's *essential*! The first, and most critical, step in dealing with the problems in your life is to take charge of the old programs that have been getting in your way.

While you're changing those old programs, if you want

226

to learn to deal with problems effectively, it helps if you have a problem-solving *method* to lead you through the process.

In this chapter, we'll deal with both of those important steps, to give you a two-part approach to solving any problem you encounter.

First, let's make sure you have the right *programs* about the way you see yourself solving problems.

GIVE YOURSELF
NEW PROGRAMS OF BELIEF

This script of Self-Talk will help you begin to believe in your own ability to get through any circumstance, and win.

Self-Talk for Solving Problems

When I have a problem, I never stop believing in my ability to solve it. I never give up, I never give in, and I always find a way.

I am creative and intelligent. If the first thing I try doesn't fix it, I think of something else.

I practice solving problems every chance I get. I don't allow myself to be discouraged by the challenges. I know I'll win, and when I do, I rejoice in my ability to get the job done.

I pay attention to the little things, so they never become big problems in the first place.

If it's my problem, I take responsibility for fixing it; if the problem belongs to someone else, I stay out of the way until that person is ready for my help.

I am never embarrassed to admit I have a problem. I help others when I can, and they are always willing to help me when I need them.

Whenever a negative situation comes up, I look first at myself to see if there is a problem with my own attitude or my behavior. If there is, I fix it, and things always get better.

If someone else has a problem that I have overcome, I am always willing to share my experience with them. I enjoy being part of a positive team.

If my idea isn't the best one, I listen and follow the better plan, no matter where it comes from. And I make sure to always give credit where it is due.

If I am unsure of my direction, I find someone who can show me the way to get back on track. I never forget there is an answer, even if I can't see it right now.

I know there is no such thing as a new problem, only a problem that is new to me. I study the ways others have conquered a similar challenge in the past, and I learn from their success.

I make a real effort to learn from my mistakes, so I don't waste time solving the same problem again.

I am good at solving problems, because I have chosen to put the right mental programs in place to help me succeed.

No problem is too difficult for me to face, or too overwhelming for me to solve. I break every problem down into steps I can manage, and take one step after another until I win.

Your problems don't have a chance, when you have *that* kind of mental strength on your side!

A PROBLEM-SOLVING SEQUENCE THAT CAN HELP

Now that I've given you some new Self-Talk to help you define your own picture of yourself as a woman who *naturally* solves problems easily, let's take a look at a step-by-step problem-solving method to help you put those programs into practice.

You can use the following list of simple steps anytime you face a difficult situation. It will lead you step by step to the point where you can actually *do* something to solve the problem.

1. **Identify the problem, and the desired result of solving it.** Take out a piece of paper, and in your own

229

words, write down what you think the problem is and what you'd like to have happen when it is solved. Keep it as simple and specific as you can, and bear in mind that as you go through the remaining steps of solving your problem, your initial view of what the problem is may very well change.

A sample problem statement would look something like this: "My husband and I are due for a tax refund. He wants to use the money for a new piano, and I've got my heart set on new carpeting for the house."

The desired result: "I want us both to be happy; I know he really cares about the piano, but I care about the carpeting, too."

2. Gather information about the problem. Mentally walk all the way around the problem and try to see it from every side. If your problem is a conflict with another person, this is the step where you try to see it from the other person's point of view. Write down everything you think you know about your situation and what is going on, including what you think is the cause of the problem itself.

In our example, your notes could include the following:

"We both have good jobs, but there's not enough money from the refund to pay for both the piano and the carpeting."

"I care about my husband's feelings, and I'd like to be able to get him the piano."

"Our carpeting is in bad shape and really needs to be replaced."

3. Develop courses of action. List your options. In any situation, you usually have more than one road to take.

The difficulty comes from trying to rush through this part of the process and make a decision before you've examined all your options. Unless it's an emergency, time is on your side. Write down every choice of action you can think of, even those scenarios you are convinced will not work out for you. Sometimes the best solution is one that you would normally have rejected. List as many options as you can.

The sample option list would look like this:

"1. I could insist on the carpeting, and try to talk my husband into waiting for his piano."

"2. I could give in, buy my husband the piano, and try not to think about the way the floor looks until next year."

"3. We could buy the carpeting, make a down payment on the piano, and make payments to pay off the piano."

"4. We could buy the piano now, and I could save money from my job to get the carpeting later."

4. Analyze the options. In this step, you'll compare the probable outcomes of each option you listed in the previous step. Write down what will most likely happen next if you make each choice. At this point, certain courses of action should begin to look more appealing than others, and some will clearly eliminate themselves from the list.

This could sound complicated, but it isn't. Let's continue with our sample problem to get an idea of how this step works.

"Option 1—If I hold out for the carpeting, I would be being selfish, and I don't want my husband to be unhappy. I don't want him to have to wait for the piano."

"Option 2—If I have to wait for new carpeting until next year's tax check comes in, *I'll* be unhappy. It's past time to do something with the floor."

"Option 3—I like this one better, but I don't really want to commit to making payments on the piano. We've just gotten to the point where our debt is in good shape, and I don't want to run up a bill."

"Option 4—I could talk to my husband and see if he would mind my saving part of my paycheck toward new carpeting. It would mean doing without other extras for a while, like eating out on weekends, but he might agree. This one could work."

5. Select an option. Make a choice. In most cases, one course of action will stand out from the others as your best choice. Even if this is not the case, and no option looks better than the next, *pick one.* The point that stops most people is when they can't decide what to do next. It's true that sometimes "doing nothing" is the best option, but only if you've *chosen* that as the best possible course of action. Don't just "do nothing" by accident; it probably won't work very well, if you do.

For now, let's say you choose Option 4.

6. Make a plan. This step is similar to listing your action steps when you are setting your goals. One by one, list each step involved in making your plan work. Start at the beginning, and follow through to the point where the problem is gone, no matter how long the list of steps may be. You'll find it's usually a much shorter list than you had imagined.

Our sample plan would include these steps:

"Step 1. Talk to my husband."

"Step 2. Get prices on piano and carpeting."
"Step 3. Choose the piano and the carpeting we want."
"Step 4. Figure out how much, if any, would be left over from the refund after we pay for the piano."
"Step 5. Determine how long it would take for me to save the rest of the money to pay for the carpeting."
"Step 6. Buy the piano."
"Step 7. Save the money for the carpeting."
"Step 8. Buy the carpeting and have it installed."

7. Put your plan into motion. Now take action. Start with step one of your plan, and *do it*. Then move on to the next step, and then the next, until you've completed the process, or it becomes clear to you that you've chosen a course of action that isn't working. Remember to give the process time, though, and don't expect your problem to vanish overnight.

In our example, as soon as you completed your list of steps, you would come up with a time to talk the problem over with your husband, and go from there.

8. Evaluate your progress. As you go through your plan, periodically stop and measure how well you're doing. You'll be able to tell fairly soon whether you are on the right course, whether things are getting better or worse. If it seems like you're on track, you probably are. If you see no hope of your plan working, go back to Step 5 and choose another option. Make a new plan with a new set of steps, and repeat the process.

In this case, Option 4 is working.

9. Give yourself *extra* programs of confidence and self-belief. It's essential to have the right Self-Talk on your side, especially when you're in a difficult situation that you're trying to improve. The more new mental programs you build that help you become a person who solves problems easily, the better you'll become at dealing with any problem that comes your way. If you don't change your old programs, you'll end up facing, and being defeated by, the same problems over and over.

Suppose it takes you four months to save enough money for the new carpeting. That's four months of looking at the floor, four months of tripping over the ragged edge of the living room carpet, and four months of hoping no one notices how bad the floor looks when they visit.

New Self-Talk programs like those for reducing stress, dealing with finances, building self-esteem, reaching goals, and improving family relationships can help you get through the difficult moments on the way to solving this sample problem.

10. Stay with it. Most people fail because they stop too soon. This is where your plan and your action steps can help you most! It's easier to stay on course when you can see exactly what's involved in getting where you're going. Combine a good plan with the right mental programs and strong determination to succeed, and you will win.

IT GETS EVEN EASIER AS YOU GO

It isn't difficult to immediately understand every aspect of this problem-solving method, even on your first time through it. What you should have gained by now is an awareness that *any* problem you have can benefit from an easy step-by-step solving process like this one, in combination with the right new mental programs to help you build belief in your own ability to overcome your challenges.

The real benefit of learning this method will come later, as you go through your daily life. You can use this same method again and again, solving problem after problem, building program after program of success, until the thought process involved becomes natural and automatic.

The secret to defeating any problem before it defeats you is simple. The solution lies in your ability to see yourself being able to cut the problem down to size, so you can break it down into a manageable series of steps that you can then deal with one at a time.

In that regard, the process of solving a problem is much like the process of reaching a goal—you do them both, one step at a time. The same rule applies for both: if you divide, you can conquer.

The more you practice solving problems, the stronger your programs will be, and the easier it will be for you.

There is one final area of Self-Talk to cover before we move on to the action chapter that will give you specific ideas on how to put your new mental programs in place right away. This final area is one of the most important, especially for women, because it deals with the way you interact with the other people in your life.

*Good communication
is the exchange
of your best thoughts and ideas.*

*Practice filling your mind
with the kind of programs
that present you
at your very best.*

Chapter 20

SELF-TALK FOR COMMUNICATION

*I*f you want to be a better communicator, there's really only one thing you need to be aware of and remember. When you're talking to another person, what you're actually doing is talking to that person's *programs*. How well the communication goes will depend in large part on the programs *they* have, and the programs *you* have.

For example, let's say you and your husband are about to have an argument about a subject you've disagreed about in the past. In this case, we'll use the topic of something as simple as "how we get from home to the airport."

The two of you are in the car, and he's driving. You're running late, and you need to get to the airport right away to pick up a friend from out of town. Your stress is already high, because it's an unexpected visit and the house isn't as neat as you'd like it to be. There's not much food in the house, either, because your weekly shopping day isn't until tomorrow, but you want to make your friend feel welcome, and you would prefer to cook dinner at home tonight.

It's 5:30 in the evening, and the roads are crowded with rush-hour traffic. Your heart sinks when you see that your husband is about to make the turn onto the multi-lane expressway to the airport, because that road makes you nervous at the best of times, and you know that there are a lot of accidents during rush hour on that particular section of road. You'd much prefer to take the side streets, even though it might take a few minutes longer to get there, because you know it's a safer route.

WHEN IN DOUBT, FIGURE IT OUT

At this point, you have two choices. You can say something to your husband about his choice of routes to take to the airport, or you can choose to avoid the issue. You can tell from the look on his face when he glances at you as he signals for the turn onto the expressway that he's expecting you to bring it up. The two of you have "been here" before, more than once, and the situation usually deteriorates badly from here.

If you want the situation to turn out in your favor, this is a great time to practice good communication skills. In spite of your emotions or your stress level, stop a moment and think about *his* computer control center, and which of *his* program files are operating at that moment.

First, he is a man (with all the programs about what being a man represents to *him*), and *he* is driving. That, at least in *his* mind, entitles him to be the one who chooses which road to take. His programs of being a good provider and protector of his wife are running at full strength. His own stress level is already elevated, just like yours, because he, too, knows the visit was unexpected, and he'd really rather have spent the evening catching up on some work from the office, as he had planned.

The *last* thing he needs at this moment is for you to say something that, from his point of view, would question his intelligence, control of the situation, or ability to manage a motor vehicle in heavy traffic. It may be hard to keep silent on the subject, especially if you're normally the kind of woman who speaks your mind and you're convinced your way is better. But an argument at this stage will only make things worse.

So if you can't do what you want to do and be a back-seat driver in order to make sure you've done all you can to see that you arrive at the airport in one piece, *what can you do?*

TAKE THE OPPORTUNITY TO TYPE IN A GOOD PROGRAM

One obvious choice would be to say nothing. But is that really the best way to communicate? It may not be, especially if your husband will interpret your silence as resentment or anger, even if you're just trying to improve the situation.

A better idea would be to figure out exactly what you can say that will give him a *positive program* when he needs it the most! It's not necessary to lie or pretend to believe something you don't. But you can easily say something *true* like, "Honey, you're really a good driver. I always feel safe with you behind the wheel."

You don't have to bring up how nervous the traffic makes you—he already *knows* that. Just give him the good program, and let it stand.

Once he's had time to process his surprise, *close* the file drawers that were open expecting to receive criticism, and *open* the right file drawers to program in what you said instead, he'll say something in response. And because you took the initiative to turn the communication around, the chances are very good that what he says next will be something *you* want to hear, instead of something you *don't.*

The thing to remember, no matter what he says next, is that you're talking to his programs, and he's talking to yours. That can go a long way toward getting rid of any resentment or animosity on either side, and help both of you set up a positive cycle that will make the visit easier on everybody.

WHAT IF YOU'RE NOT YET THE KIND OF COMMUNICATOR YOU OUGHT TO BE?

I gave you that simple example to illustrate an important point. In order to be a good communicator about *anything*, with *anyone*, you have to do more than consider the other person's point of view. You have to consider the other person's *programs*, whatever they may be.

Few of us are as skilled in the area of communication as we would like to be. Some women would like to be able to be more assertive and expressive in conversation. Others know they don't listen as carefully as they could, and those women who talk too much are more than likely aware they have that habit.

No matter where you fall on that conversational scale, the right programs of Self-Talk are essential to being a good communicator. Even if you're already comfortable with your skills in this area, you can benefit from the knowledge that in order to truly understand how human communication works, you have to look at it from the standpoint of programming.

If you learn programs like these, you'll be more at ease and confident in any situation that involves talking with and understanding other people.

Self-Talk for Communication

I am a good communicator. I think well, I express myself clearly, and I stay on the subject.

I know that good communication is the exchange of thoughts and ideas, so I practice filling my mind with the kind of programs that present me at my very best.

I have learned to listen, and I practice good listening habits every chance I get.

I never forget that when I'm listening to others, what I'm really hearing is their programs—and I respond accordingly.

I recognize the power of a sincere compliment, and I often take the time to let others know what I like about them.

When I am talking to people, I meet their eyes. My confidence tells them I am truly interested in what they have to say.

I listen more than I talk.

I wait until it is my turn to talk, and I never use my listening time to practice what I'm going to say next. When I listen, I <u>listen</u>.

Whenever I am asked for advice, I never forget that less is more, and I keep my remarks to a minimum.

I never gossip.

Whenever I speak, my smile says the most about me.

I learn everything I can, every chance I get. I do what I need to do to be an interesting person.

If I don't know something, I admit it. When I do know something, I express myself clearly and with confidence.

I see everyone I meet as a potential new friend. I never hesitate to be the first to start a conversation.

My life is better because I take the time to be interested in many things.

I never miss an opportunity to find out how to improve myself. If someone is doing it right, I ask them to teach me what they know, and I practice what I learn.

I am always willing to share my knowledge and talents with others who are interested in me.

When I am talking with someone else, I ignore distractions. I let them know they are important enough to deserve my full attention.

People like to listen to me, because I make sure that when I talk, I have something to say. I have mastered the art of good communication, and it shows!

The secret to good communication, as with mastering each of the other areas we've looked at in the Self-Talk sections, is to understand the fine art of programming so that you can use it to improve your life.

In the next part of the book, we're going to go over tips and techniques for putting what you've learned about Self-Talk and programming into practice right away. This next and final section deals with how you can *take action now*.

Part IV
PROGRAMMING YOURSELF
FOR SUCCESS

*Each positive new program
you get
has a way of reinforcing
the good programs
you already have
in the other areas
of your life.*

*If you don't know
where to start,
<u>start anywhere.</u>*

Chapter 21

TAKING ACTION NOW

*I*t's always good to learn new things, and learning about Self-Talk and how programming works is no exception. But the *best* part is what happens when you *use* what you've learned.

This is your opportunity to put Self-Talk into practice! In this chapter, you'll learn specific ways to change your old programs and make your new Self-Talk a permanent and natural part of who you are.

How much or little you decide to change is up to you. Now that you've gone through the twelve main areas of your programs about who you are and what you do, you should have a good idea of which areas of your programs you'd like to work on most. And by the way, if it seems like *all* your programs need work, don't despair. Each new program you get in *one* area has a way of reinforcing the good programs you have in the *other* areas of your life. If you don't know where to start, start anywhere.

In this part of the book, I share with you the best of what I've learned from nearly ten years of helping people change their programs with Self-Talk. I have seen each of the methods in action, and I know from personal experience that the techniques I've presented here can make a real difference in your life, if you choose to use them.

CHANGING YOUR PROGRAMS WITH SELF-TALK

In an earlier chapter, I mentioned the four steps involved in changing your programs: to *monitor* your current programs to find out what they are, to *edit* anytime you're about to type in a new program, to make the decision to *reprogram* by building new mental highways and breaking the old ones down, and to *practice* what you've learned until it becomes a new habit.

In this section, I'm going to share with you the best of the ideas and methods in those four areas. As a first step, we'll take a look at the programs you *already* have.

Step #1:
MONITORING

1. Listen to everything you say out loud, and everything you think.

The monitoring process begins with listening to yourself. Once you become aware of the way you sound, you can get a remarkably clear picture of what your programs are. It's a good idea to ask someone close to you to write down some of the program statements you say most often. That list may surprise you.

2. Listen to the programs of the people around you.

Don't tell them what they're doing wrong, or that they need to get new Self-Talk programs. Few people I know will thank you for that advice. We'll discuss ways to help them later; for now, just *listen*.

3. Compare the person to their programs.

As you monitor, notice which people are more effective or successful than others. You should begin to see a connection. The people who do the best are the ones who have the best *programs* working for them. The ones who don't do as well will sound completely different, because their programs need work.

4. Take a close look at the input you get from media.

You're getting new programs every time you read a book or a magazine, listen to the radio, or watch TV. As you become aware of what the right and wrong kinds of programs sound like, pay attention to everything you read, see, or hear. Think of each input as someone typing a program into your mental computer, a program that will eventually vote for or against you.

5. Make a list of positive sources of programs, and a list of negative sources.

Which people do you know who give you the best input? What television or radio programs can you tune in to that will build good programs for you, or enhance the ones you already have? Which ones give you programs that are unhealthy, depressing, mindless, or pointless? Which types of books should you read to build successful new program pathways, and which would be better left alone?

6. Make a separate list of those input sources you'd *like* to have in your life, but currently don't.

This could be spending time with a person you'd like to pattern yourself after as a mentor, a place you'd like to visit that will expand your mind or teach you something new, a college course you've always wanted to take, or a new category of books or videos that will give you programs of success and effectiveness. Make your list as long as you can, and add to it often.

Step #2:
EDITING

1. Begin to change what you say, and what you think.

Change it. Turn it around. If you are about to say or think a program that you know will work against you, give yourself a mental override. Take manual control of your keyboard, go off autopilot for a moment, and say or think the mental program you know will work better.

2. *Carefully* explain to others that you'd prefer the right input.

249

Walk on eggs with this one. People don't like to be told how they should—or *shouldn't*—express themselves, least of all people whose own old programs allow them to say things to you that are less than helpful in the first place! You can find a way to gently let them know that your programs and your future are important to you, and tell them how they can play a positive role that will support you in your growth by changing what they say to you, about you.

3. Stop inviting or allowing outside negative input.

Get rid of the sources of bad news that you don't need to see or hear in your life. If a program on television carries a warning sticker that tells you it's bad input for your kids, that should signal *you* that your time might be better spent elsewhere. If you're spending time with the wrong people simply because that's what you've always done and you have a history together, rewrite the next chapter of your own biography by finding better friends. Eliminate every source of negative input you can, and your new programs will have a much better chance.

4. Find a way to get your own attention, every time you repeat the wrong program.

One woman told me she saved enough for a vacation, just by having her kids collect ten dollars for the savings account every time they heard her say a negative program. "I did really well with that," she said, laughing. "I was down to ten bucks a *week* after the first two weeks!"

5. Remind yourself frequently that *you* are the one in charge of your keyboard.

The rest of the world will never stop giving you programs, or at least *trying* to. Until the day when everyone has only the right programs to repeat and pass on to you, it's a good idea to take personal responsibility for every input you get. You can stop negative or harmful input simply by refusing to accept it, and by *immediately* replacing it with something better.

6. Have several favorite lines of Self-Talk ready when you need them.

When you hear or see the wrong program, *instantly* repeat a program statement that works in your favor. Athletes do it, doctors do it, pilots do it, and you can, too. One good method is to visualize the harmful program as if you're looking at it through a window. Mentally drop a window shade to block out the wrong input, and turn to face another window where you can clearly see a visual image of a new program of the right kind to help you win.

Step #3:
REPROGRAMMING

1. Familiarize yourself with the way your programs *ought* to sound.

By reading the Self-Talk chapters in this book, you've made a good start in the right direction. The better you are at recognizing good input when you hear it, the easier and more natural it will be for you to build programs of the right kind.

2. Read the Self-Talk scripts in this book.

Keep the Self-Talk scripts handy, so you can read them again each time you face a situation from a particular programming area. Don't worry if you don't have time to read them every day. The goal of Self-Talk is *not* to complicate your life, but to make it work better for you. Read them when you need to, when you want to, and when you can. Remember that every time you do, you're repeating programs and feeding the right new highways in your brain. The more often you program in the new Self-Talk, the better it works.

3. Listen to Self-Talk Cassettes.

The reason the professionally recorded tapes of the Self-Talk scripts are so popular is a simple one. You can change your programs *while you're busy doing the same things you normally do.* (Although they are *not* any kind of hypnosis or "subliminal" tapes, Self-Talk tapes work best when you listen to them in the background, while you're doing something else.) Remember, any change that is too difficult, radical, or drastic won't last very long. Adding the Self-Talk in this way is an easy change.

That convenience can make a critical difference in whether you change your programs, or not. The reason I recommend the professional versions rather than home-made ones is also simple: *they work.* If you try to make tapes in your own voice or have a friend do it, you either never get around to it, or you hate the way they sound, or you end up listening to the voice of your own worst critic—*you*. Also, it's very important that when it comes to programs, you give yourself the real thing, done in the right way.

4. Surround yourself with success.

Your *environment* plays a crucial role in the programs you get. By environment, I mean everyone you come in contact with, all those objects you choose to have around you, where you choose to spend your time, and every source of input you give yourself. Make it a point to surround yourself with the best. Program yourself with *quality* and *character*, in every way you can. Spend your time with people you respect and admire; keep your house and even your car in order; listen to uplifting music, and put beauty into your daily view every chance you get. Your programs will follow suit.

5. Set a goal to do everything you need to do to change your programs.

This step will get you started, and keep you moving in the right direction. If you have a solid *goal* to change your programs, instead of a vague *wish* or *desire* to improve, you have a much better chance of getting past the old mental highways that have been holding you back. While you're at it, give yourself some other positive goals to work toward. The choice to set a goal and do something with it will give you a positive program beginning *now*, and set up a pattern of success and high self-esteem for your new programs to build on.

6. Reward yourself when you do it right.

Just as it helps to get your own attention when you get it *wrong*, set up a system to notify you when you do it *right*. We all thrive on appreciation and applause, and our programs get even better when we are rewarded. Your reward could be a new book, a lunch or dinner out, or simply an extra half-hour of sleep on Saturday morning. Do what it takes to set a positive reward cycle in motion that works for *you*, based on what makes *you* feel great about yourself. Use a good program—reward yourself—that builds another good program—which leads to another reward, and so on. After that, as we discussed earlier, the exciting part happens when the Self-Talk cycle takes off on its own.

Step #4:
PRACTICING

1. Set a schedule to work on your new Self-Talk.

This one is easy when you're using tapes, because they are designed specifically to be listened to every day. But even if you choose not to do that, it's essential to give yourself repetition of your new programs. In order to build the new habits fast, a schedule works best. If you're reading the Self-Talk scripts, try to read them the same time each day. The same goes if you choose to get good input from reading positive or uplifting books, or watching an educational videotape. Set aside a time each day, or each week, to work on building new programs.

2. Find someone else to work on Self-Talk with you.

The partner system works especially well when it comes to making the decision to change your old programs. It's a lot more fun. Most women don't even like to go to the bathroom in a strange restaurant by themselves, so why should you try to work on your Self-Talk without support from your friends or family? The more people in your life who are aware of programming and what you're trying to do with it, the simpler and easier it will be for you to make the positive changes in your life that you're looking for.

3. Share what you've learned with someone else.

Again, this is not intended to be used in a negative, critical or nagging way, or as an excuse to tell others what they're doing wrong. It can be incredibly exciting, though, to share the positive truth about programming with other people. My favorite is to work with children, showing them how they can build healthy self-esteem and reach for their dreams. Kids these days understand computers even better than we do, so they quickly understand programming, and they're hungry to hear good things about their potential to achieve.

If you want to brighten your day and someone else's, and reinforce your new Self-Talk knowledge in the process, share the word.

4. Stay with it, and don't stop.

Remember, it takes a minimum of about 3 weeks of staying off an old program path for that highway in the brain to even *begin* to break down. Don't worry if you don't instantly see an overnight success that transforms your life! The real impact of your new programs will be seen and felt in the next weeks and months and *years* of your life. You *can* and *should* start to notice benefit right away, but the longer you work on building the right programs, the easier and more effective it will be.

You do get programmed, as we all do, but you *don't* have to *keep* the programs you've gotten along the way. You can change them. I encourage you to make the decision to once and for all take charge of your own mental keyboard, so that never again will you allow anyone to program *you* with less than the best.

If you use the techniques and the Self-Talk you've learned in this book, *your programs will change.* Use the techniques. Practice giving yourself the *right* programs, and the *wrong* ones will lose their hold on your life.

Believe in your dream. If you don't remember what that dream is, or if you've never taken the time to figure out what it might be, now is the time to think about that. Once you decide on your dream, you can apply the solid techniques of goal-setting from this book to put you on the right path to take you there.

The *ultimate* goal is to get rid of all the old programs that work against you, and *replace* them with a new set of mental highways that can take you at high speed toward your future. And the most important thing to remember about changing your programs with Self-Talk is this: *if you want to, you can.*

*You can become
the kind of woman
you'd most like to be.*

*Your new Self-Talk,
and what you do
to change your programs,
is the key.*

Chapter 22

WHERE DO YOU GO FROM HERE?

I'm the kind of person who hates to say goodbye, and I've been known to come back for one more hug or another smile of encouragement when you least expect it.

By now, I hope I've given you new insight on your own potential and possibility, and shown you that you *can*, and *deserve to*, become the kind of woman you'd most like to be. I would give anything in my power to be able to find a way to unlock that door for you, the barrier between where you are now and where you want to go in your life.

It should be clear to you by this point that I'm convinced Self-Talk, and changing your programs, holds that key.

In spite of all my attempts to be logical and clear and easy to understand, the truth is this: I lead with my heart.

So wherever you are, whoever you are, and whatever you believe yourself to be capable of at the moment, remember this:

I believe in you.

I will never stop believing in you. I will never falter, or fall back, or become convinced you are less than I know you are: a wonderful, strong, beautiful woman with more to offer this world than you might ever have imagined.

You can't stop me. No matter where you go, no matter what you do next, whether you choose to change your programs or not (although I hope and believe you *will*), never forget that somewhere out there is a person who sees who you *really* are—and likes what she sees.

If I could give you one gift, it would be the ability to once and for all see yourself the way I do, and begin to believe what you *can* do with the life you have been given. This book is that gift to you.

I hope it takes you where you want to go.

Professional Self-Talk Cassettes of the Self-Talk scripts appearing in this book may be ordered directly from the publisher by calling:

1-800-982-8196

or by writing to:

Self-Talk Information Services
P.O. Box 65659
Tucson, AZ 85728

To contact Elise Thomas Helmstetter, write:
c/o P.O. Box 65659
Tucson, AZ 85728